The Gift of Trout

Books by Ted Leeson

The Habit of Rivers

The Gift of Trout (editor)

The Gift of Trout

Edited by Ted Leeson

A Trout Unlimited Book

Afterword by Charles Gauvin
Illustrations by Gordon Allen

Lyons & Burford, Publishers

Printed in the United States of America
This book is printed on acid-free and process chlorine-free paper.

10 9 8 7 6 5 4 3 2 1

Design by Elaine Streithof

Library of Congress Cataloging-in-Publication Data

The gift of trout / edited by Ted Leeson ; afterword by Charles Gauvin; illustrations by Gordon Allen.
   p.   cm.
   "A Trout Unlimited book."
   ISBN 1-55821-477-1
   1. Trout fishing.   I. Leeson, Ted.
SH687.G55 1996
799.1'755—dc20

Table of Contents

Introduction

Ted Leeson

EVERY ANGLER, I think, pursues the sport inside a set of privately drawn boundaries, and for some of us—the most fortunate, we would claim—the borders we construct have a distinctly trout-shaped contour. Our selection of tackle and methods, our choice of places and times, the terms in which we define our hopes and gauge success—all stake out a space that is the wonderful geography of trout fishing, and we tend to explore it with a zeal far out of proportion to any statistical significance of the object. Trout are neither the largest of species nor the smallest, the most common or rare, the most widespread or localized, the easiest to catch or the most difficult. By any such measures, trout are an undistinguished fish, and to the dispassionate eye of the non-angler, our obsession must seem a puzzling and wholly arbitrary predilection. And in many ways, none of them particularly important, this is probably true and most certainly beside the point. We are drawn to trout by the magnetism of intuition or instinct, and any attempt to explain it is bound to seem a lame, after-the-fact rationalization in the eyes of the unconverted—which I suppose is why they don't fish in the first place.

To trout anglers, of course, it all makes perfect sense, though one that is not easily articulated. Ask them about their strange fascination with trout and almost immediately the talk will turn to other things—rivers and landscapes, insects and hatches, solitude and solace, rods, flies, the love of place, the endless hope held by water upstream. And if there is any common denominator among these apparently tangential matters, it is exactly that they are tangential. Though not about, or directly about, fish, they are still somehow connected to trout. And this very connectedness, I believe, is what underlies the passion for fishing. Trout themselves are infinitely fascinating creatures, but no one (at least no one I know) would get very excited at the prospect of fishing the pellet-stuffed imposters that mill around in concrete stew ponds. What is as important as the trout is that trout-shaped space that we carve out around it, for the two are finally indistinguishable in the angler's eyes. Trout do not exist alone and intact in the psychic or aesthetic sense any more than they do in the biological one. As the mathematician would say, trout are a necessary, but not sufficient, condition—though vital to our pleasure and interest and wonder, the fish in and of themselves are unable to account for these things completely. Trout are much more than simply an occasion for our passion, but less than its sole source.

All of which is to say that our appreciation of trout is, in great measure, contextual. The trout is inseparable from larger and more inclusive worlds; it is a fact of biology at the center of an intricate and expansive system of connections—to the intriguing, half-understood universe of a trout stream; to the entire natural world; to an historical tradition; an ethic; a social and environmental responsibility; to personal meanings; and to a thousand other things of value. *Trout* is simply a kind of angler's shorthand that invokes all of these significances.

This book celebrates trout by attempting to decipher the shorthand—to explore in the work of some of angling's best writers the abundance and variety of contexts that create the trout angler's world. The editorial principles that governed the selections for this volume were simple and specific. I sought out first-rate writing that explored the ways in which trout are connected—at times directly, at other times subtly, at still others quite personally—to other parts of our experience. What I found was an embarrassment of riches, and for all the usual logistical reasons—length, availability, duplication of material, space—some fine writers and writing were, with the greatest reluctance, omitted from this volume. It may be the inevitable fate of any anthologist to brood over what had to be excluded, but in the end my regrets are overshadowed by the wonder and pleasure of the pieces contained here. They represent a broad diversity of perspectives, from angles both familiar and unusual that, in aggregate, suggest the richly textured, three-dimensional world that surrounds the trout.

The first essay here, David Quammen's "Synecdoche and the Trout," investigates the very idea of connectedness itself. The trout, he says, is a kind of metaphor that represents both itself and a host of significances joined to, but outside, itself. As this idea becomes the premise for his own inquiry into those connections, so it serves as an introduction to the rest of the pieces in this collection, which undertake a similar search.

Paul Schullery's piece, "Early American Trout Fishing," chronicles the beginning of the sport in this country and suggests how the specific shape of American trout fishing developed as a response both to social and particularly to geographical contexts—it is, he observes, to the "rich variety of waters that we owe the remarkable diversity of our fishing tradition."

In "Blue Ridge Complex," Christopher Camuto addresses on a more intimate scale the connection between fish and country and history. "No doubt," he writes, "it is an accident of design, but the convoluted ribbing of contour lines on the topographic maps reminds me of the vermiculation on a brook trout's back and makes some important connections between land and trout clear." The "worm-like tracings" on the trout lead to old maps and finally to William Byrd's *History of the Dividing Line* in a rumination that explores the ways in which both trout and history are expressions of landscape.

As the pursuit of trout has national beginnings and regional significances, so it has private and personal ones. David James Duncan recounts, in "First Native," the mystical, electric, transforming moment of catching his first wild trout, of feeling "the sudden life pulsing, punching, shouting clean into the marrow of my know-nothing, nine-year-old hands. . . . Neither my hands, nor I, have been quite the same since."

Lorian Hemingway describes in her essay "Walk on Water for Me" this same instant of psychic change and redemption, experienced at a point much later in life. It is for her both a moment of new understanding and a return to the half-forgotten knowledge of childhood, a wonderful recognition of how the past and present reciprocally shed light on one another.

A somewhat different insight into personal beginnings takes shape in Marjorie Sandor's "The Novitiate's Tale"—the new fly fisher's initiatory quest into the funny, contradictory, perpetually bewildering world of what anglers possess in greatest abundance: advice. And not even the worst of it can prevent the fly-fishing passion from being born in one so irrepressibly predisposed to it: "Suffice it to say," she writes, "that though I fished the wrong spot all day, with the wrong line and the wrong fly, the Bitterroot itself, with its willow-shaded margins and islands, its riffles and runs and promising boulders all just out of reach, made failure seem both a reasonable and sublime occupation."

This notion, that "fly fishing for trout is a sport that depends not so much on catching the fish as on their mere presence," as John Gierach puts it in his aptly titled "Trout," suggests that the very idea of trout, especially large ones, compels the angler. "Although individual fish clearly exist" he writes, "*The Trout*, remains a legendary creature," and his essay, with characteristic wit and irony, comments on both the fish and our ideas about them.

One such idea, "selectivity," is investigated by Datus Proper in "The Best Thing About Trout." In his wry but closely reasoned piece, he uses the facts of fish biology and behavior to dissect the conventional beliefs that surround trout. And if he does not entirely demolish the sacred cow of selective trout, he makes hamburger of much of it, and suggests that, in the end, some of our criteria for choosing fly patterns serve mostly to provide "moral comfort" to ourselves, "which," he concedes, "is a very important feature in trout flies."

If the trout seen by Gierach and Proper—as a compelling idea, as a problem to be solved—accounts for the way we approach our fishing, it is the connection of trout to particular places that accounts for so much of our pleasure. In "Hot Creek," Michael Checchio travels to California's Owens Valley, scene of the most shameless water piracy in national history. Amid this landscape of "lost possibility," he discovers that not quite all has been lost. Wild trout endure, and in the face of such things, he observes, "you wonder just what it is you have done right with your life to deserve such a gift."

More remote places and lesser-known trout are the subject of Roderick Haig-Brown's "Sea-Run Cutthroats." In the coastal rivers of British Columbia, he pursues this "down-to-earth, workaday" fish, a trout that lives "in his own place in his own way and has his own special virtues"—all of which Haig-Brown describes with thoughtfulness, intelligence, and affection.

The particular place for John Engels is the water below the Soo locks. In his haunting poem, "Big Water," it was the large rainbows, he says,

> . . . That kept us coming back
> five years more at least, though between us
> we caught exactly nothing, *half*

> *of nothing apiece,* my brother said,
> and we worked hard for it.

And these uncaught trout become the vantage point from which to survey both hope and things lost.

Trout streams are, of course, specific physical places, but they are psychological spaces as well. In " Karen's Pool," Harry Middleton surveys the geography of memory. Running through the middle of it all, he finds Starlight Creek, the vital nerve of his boyhood that energizes one small part of the world, making it "sensible and full of purpose."

In Thomas McGuane's "Midstream," trout water provides a somewhat different point of vantage. "Mortality being what it is," he notes, "any new river could be your last"—a notion that produces, among other things, "a sweet and consoling inventory of all the previous rivers in your life." Midstream is a literal and figurative place to stand and assess just what you might have learned from rivers and trout. My own contribution, "On the Take," examines perhaps the most visual and dramatic way in which that learning takes place—dry-fly fishing. To drift a floating fly is to place a question, a conjecture on the surface of the water. The rise of a trout is a question answered, a surmise confirmed, one small but important thing learned about a river.

Many anglers do nearly as much angling in books as they do in streams; some of our most memorable trout and trout places are made of words. In his essay "At the Second Bend Pool," Nick Lyons takes time during the fishing to reflect on a lifetime spent searching for words in which to speak about trout fishing, a language that is as faithful to the creature and the occupation as it is to himself. Bob Berls casts a wider net in "Sudden Spate," where he delves into the literature of fly fishing and emerges with an armload of books that represent the best works on fly fishing to appear in the last thirty years.

I began by saying that the trout angler's passion for trout is largely a matter of private inclination and personal taste. But it is not entirely so. Trout are taking on an increasingly public significance. Because of their exacting biological requirements for clean, cold, pure water, and lots of it, trout have become an emblem not only of environmental quality, but of national attitudes toward the natural world and the policies that alter it. There is no such thing anymore as a non-political trout. I think that some part of nearly every angler's attachment to trout and trout fishing stems from this immediate concern—that the fate of trout in some measure reflects the fate of our world. Its health is an index of our own biological and ethical well-being, and the connection is worth preserving. "If the trout are lost," writes McGuane, "smash the state."

Many of the selections in this book touch on environmental matters, but two of the pieces here address them quite specifically. In "Can Fly Fishing Survive the Twenty-first Century?" George Anderson assesses the ways in which we, as fishermen, bear some responsibility for the conditions of our trout streams and speculates about what might be required in the upcoming century to preserve the quality of both the fishing and the experience of being astream. William McLarney's "Who Says They Don't Make Trout Streams Anymore?" chronicles one of the rare success stories that are cause for hope—the restoration of Cape Cod's Quashnet River as a sea-run trout stream. In the process, the stream-fixers find themselves "dealing, not only with trout habitat, but with wildlife, marine issues, open space concerns, drinking water, and Indian land rights." They discover, in short, the deep interconnectedness of the trout to things both near and remote.

As perceptive and illuminating as these writers are, this collection is, in the end, only suggestive. The deep attraction for trout and trout fishing is that they will forever contain their measures of mystery, and the whole will always exceed the sum of its parts. It is, perhaps, the reason we fish in the first place.

Synecdoche and the Trout

David Quammen

IT IS A SIMPLE QUESTION with a seemingly simple answer. "Why do you live in *Montana*?"

Repeatedly over a span of thirteen years you have heard this, asked most often by people who know you just well enough to be aware of the city where you grew up, the tony universities you attended, and a few other bits of biographic detail on the basis of which they harbor a notion that you should have taken your place in New York café society or, at least, an ivy-adorned department of English. They suspect you, these friends do, of hiding out. Maybe in a way they are right. But they have no clear sense of what you are hiding from, or why, let alone where. Hence their question.

"The trout," you answer, and they gape back blankly.

"The trout," they say after a moment. "That's a fish."

"Correct."

"Like lox."

"In some ways similar."

"You like to go fishing. *That's* why you live out there? *That's* why you spend your life in a place without decent restaurants or bookstores or symphony orchestras, a place halfway between Death Valley and the North Pole? A place where there's no espresso, and the *Times* comes in three days late by pontoon plane? Do I have this straight, now? It's because you like to go *fishing?*"

"No," you say. "Only partly. At the beginning, that was it, yes. But I've stayed thirteen years. No plans to leave."

"You *went* for the fishing, but you *stayed* for something else. Aha."

"Yes. The trout," you say.

"This is confusing."

"A person can get too much trout fishing. Then it cloys, becomes taken for granted. Meaningless."

"Again like lox."

"I don't seem to fish nearly as much as I used to."

"But you keep talking about the trout. You went, you stayed; the trout is your reason."

"The trout is a synecdoche," you say, because these friends are tough and verbal and they can take it.

2

A biologist would use the term "indicator species." Because I have the biases of a journalist (working that great gray zone between newspaper reporting and fiction, engaged daily in trying to make facts not just talk but yodel), I speak instead of synecdoche. We both mean that a trout represents more than itself—but that, and more important, it also does represent itself.

"A poem should not *mean* but *be,*" wrote Archibald MacLeish, knowing undeniably in his heart that a good poem quite often does both.

Likewise, a trout.

The presence of trout in a body of water is a discrete zoological fact that nevertheless signifies certain things.

It signifies a definite complex of biotic and chemical and physical factors, a standard of richness and purity, without which that troutly presence is impossible. It signifies aquatic nutrients like calcium, potassium, nitrate, phosphate; signifies enough carbon dioxide to nourish meadows of algae and keep calcium in solution as calcium bicarbonate; signifies a prolific invertebrate fauna (Plecoptera, Trichoptera, Diptera, Ephemeroptera), and a temperature regime confined within certain daily and annual extremes. It also signifies clear pools emptying down staircases of rounded boulders and dappled with patterns of late-afternoon shade cast by chrome-yellow cottonwood leaves in September. It signifies solitude so sweet and pure as to bring an ache to the sinuses, a buzz to the ears. Loneliness and anomie of the most wholesome sort. It signifies dissolved oxygen to at least four or five parts per million. It signifies a good possibility of osprey, dippers, and kingfishers, otters and water shrews, heron; and it signifies *Salmo gairdneri, Salmo clarki, Salmo trutta.* Like a well-chosen phrase in any poem, MacLeish's included, the very presence of trout signifies at more than one level. Magically, these creatures are literal and real. They live in imagination, memory, and cold water.

For instance: I can remember the first trout I ever caught as an adult (which was also the first I ever caught on a fly), and precisely what the poor little fish represented to me at that moment. It represented (a) dinner and (b) a new beginning, with a new sense of self, in a new place. The matter of dinner was important, since I was a genuinely hungry young man living out of my road-weary Volkswagen bus with a meager supply of groceries. But the matter of selfhood and place, the matter of reinventing identity, was paramount. My hands trembled wildly as I took that fish off the hook.

A rainbow, all of seven or eight inches long. A Black Gnat pattern, size 12, tied cheaply of poor materials somewhere in the Orient and picked up by me at Herter's when I had passed through South Dakota. I killed the little trout before it could slip through my fingers and, heartbreakingly, disappear. This episode was for me exactly equivalent to the one in Faulkner's "Delta Autumn," where blood from a fresh-killed buck is smeared on the face of the boy. *I slew you,* the boy thinks. *My bearing must not shame your quitting life,* he understands. *My conduct for ever onward must become your death.* In my own case, of course, there was no ancient Indian named Sam Fathers serving as mentor and baptist. I was alone and an autodidact. The blood of the little trout did not steam away its heat of life into the cold air, and I smeared none on my face. Nevertheless.

This fish came out of a creek in the Big Horn Mountains of northeastern Wyoming, and I was on my way to Montana, though at that moment I didn't yet know it.

Montana was the one place on earth farthest in miles and in spirit from Oxford University where you could still get by with the English language, and the sun didn't disappear below the horizon for days in a row during midwinter, and the prevailing notion of a fish dinner was not lutefisk. I had literally never set foot within the borders of this place called "Montana." I had no friends there, no friends of friends, no contacts of any sort, which was fine. I looked at a map and

saw jagged blue lines, denoting mountain rivers. All I knew
was that, in Montana, there would be more trout.

Trout were the indicator species for a place and a life I
was seeking.

I went. Six years later, rather to my surprise, I was a professional fishing guide under license from the Montana Department of Fish, Wildlife and Parks. My job was to smear the blood on other young
faces. *I slew you. My bearing must not shame your quitting life.* Sometimes it was actually like that, though quite often it was not.

Item. You are at the oars of a fourteen-foot Avon raft, pushing across a slow
pool on the Big Hole River in western Montana. An August afternoon. Seated in
front of you is an orthopedic surgeon from San Francisco, a pleasant man who can
talk intelligently about the career of Gifford Pinchot or the novels of Evelyn
Waugh, who is said to play a formidable game of squash, and who spends one
week of each year fishing for trout. In his right hand is a Payne bamboo rod that
is worth more than the car you drive, and attached to the rod is a Hardy Perfect
reel. At the end of the doctor's line is a kinked and truncated leader, and at the
end of the leader is a dry fly which can no longer by even the most technical definition be considered "dry," having been slapped back and forth upon and dragged
through several miles of river. With this match of equipment to finesse, the good
doctor might as well be hauling manure in the back seat of a Mercedes. Seated
behind you is the doctor's wife, who picked up a fly rod for the first time in her
life two hours earlier. Her line culminates in a fly that is more dangerous to you
than to any fish in Montana. As you have rowed quietly across the glassy pool,
she has attacked the water's surface like a French chef dicing celery.

Now your raft has approached the brink of a riffle. On the Big Hole River during this late month of the season, virtually all of the catchable trout cluster (by
daylight) where they can find cover and oxygen, in those two wedges of deep still
water flanking the fast current at the bottom of each riffle. You have told the doctor and his wife about the wedges. There, *those*, you have said. Cast just across the
eddy line, you have said. Throw a little slack. We've got to hit the spots to catch
any fish, you have said in the tactfully editorial first-person plural.

As your raft slides into this particular riffle, the doctor and his wife become
tense with anticipation. The wife snags her fly in the rail rope along the rowing
frame, and asks sweetly if you would free it, which you do, grabbing the oars again

quickly to avoid hitting a boulder. You begin working to slalom the boat through the riffle. The wife whips her fly twice through the air before sinking it into the back of your straw cowboy hat. She apologizes fervently. Meanwhile, she lets her line loop around your right oar. You take a stroke with the left oar to swing clear of a drowned log, and point your finger over the doctor's shoulder: "Remember, now. The wedges." He nods eagerly. The raft is about to broadside another boulder, so you pull hard on both oars and with that motion your hat is jerked into the river. The doctor makes five false casts, intent on the wedges, and then fires his line forward into the tip of his own rod like a handful of spaghetti hitting a kitchen wall. He moans. The raft drops neatly out of the riffle, between the wedges, and back into dead water.

Item. You are two days along on a wilderness float through the Smith River canyon, fifty miles and another three river-days from the nearest hospital, with cliffs of shale towering hundreds of feet on each side of the river to seal you in. The tents are grouped on a cottonwood flat. It is dinner hour, and you have just finished a frigid bath in the shallows. As you open your first beer, a soft-spoken Denver architect walks back into camp with a size 14 Royal Wulff stuck past the barb into his lower eyelid. He has stepped behind another fisherman at precisely the wrong moment. Everyone looks queasily at everyone else, but the outfitter— who is your boss, who is holding his second martini, and whose own nerves are already frazzled from serving as chief babysitter to eight tourist fishermen—looks pleadingly at you. With tools from your fishing vest (a small pair of scissors, a forceps, a loop of leader) you extract the fly. Then you douse the architect's wound with what little remains of the outfitter's gin.

Item. Three days down the Smith on a different trip, under a cloudless July sky, you are drifting, basking comfortably in the heat, resting your oars. In your left hand is a cold Pabst Blue Ribbon. In place of your usual tee shirt, you are wearing a new yellow number that announces with some justice: "Happiness Is a Cold Pabst." On your head, in place of the cowboy straw, is a floppy cloth porkpie in a print of Pabst labels. In the bow seat of your raft, casting contentedly to a few rising trout, is a man named Augie Pabst, scion of the family. Augie, contrary to all your expectations, is a sensitive and polite man, a likable fellow. Stowed in your cargo box and your cooler are fourteen cases of Pabst Blue Ribbon, courtesy. You take a deep gulp of beer, you touch an oar. Ah, yes, you think. Life in the wilderness.

Item. You are floating a petroleum engineer and his teenage son through the final twelve miles of the Smith canyon, which is drowsy, meandering water not hospitable to rainbow trout but good for an occasional large brown. The temperature is ninety-five, the midday glare is fierce, you have spent six days with these particular people, and you are eager to be rid of them. Three more hours to the take-out, you tell yourself. A bit later you think, Two more. The petroleum engineer has been treated routinely with ridicule by his son, and evidently has troubles also with his wife. The wife is along on this trip but she does not fish; she does not seem to talk much to her husband; she has ridden a supply boat with the outfitter and spent much of her time humming quietly. You wonder if the petroleum engineer has heard of Hemingway's Francis Macomber. You are sure that the outfitter has not and you suspect that the wife has. The engineer says that he and his son would like to catch one large brown trout before the trip ends, so you tell them to tie on Marabou muddlers and drag those billowy monstrosities through certain troughs. Fifteen minutes later, the boy catches a large brown. This fish is eighteen inches long and broad of shoulder—a noble and beautiful animal that the Smith River has taken five years to grow. The father tells you to kill it—yeah, I guess kill it—they will want to eat it, just this one, at the hotel. Suddenly you despise your job. You despise this man, but he is paying your wage and so he has certain entitlements. You kill the fish, pushing your thumb into its mouth and breaking back the neck. Its old sharp teeth cut your hand.

The boy is a bad winner, a snot, taunting his father now as the three of you float on down the river. Half an hour later, the father catches a large brown, this one also around eighteen inches. You are pleased for him, and glad for the fish, since you assume that it will go free. But the father has things to prove to the wife as well as to the son, and for the former your eyewitness testimony of a great battle, a great victory, and a great act of mercy will not suffice. "Better keep this one, too," he says, "and we'll have a pair." You detest this particular euphemistic use of the word "keep." You argue tactfully but he pretends not to hear. Your feelings for these trout are what originally brought you out onto the Smith River and are what compel you to bear the company of folk like the man and his son. *My conduct for ever onward must become your death.* The five-year-old brown trout is lambent, spotted with orange, lithe as an ocelot, swirling gorgeously under water in your gentle grip. You kill it.

I don't guide anymore. I haven't renewed my license in a handful of years. My early and ingenuous ideas about the role of a fishing guide turned out to be totally wrong: I had imagined it as a life rich with independence, and with a rustic sort of dignity, wherein a fellow would stand closer to these particular animals he admired inordinately. I hadn't foreseen that it would demand the humility of a chauffeur and the complaisance of a pimp.

And I don't seem to fish nearly as much as I used to. I have a dilemma these days: I dislike killing trout but I believe that, in order to fish responsibly, to fish conscionably, the fisherman should at least occasionally kill. Otherwise he can too easily delude himself that fly fishing is merely a game, a dance of love, played in mutual volition and mutual empathy by the fisherman and the trout. Small flies with the barbs flattened are an excellent means for allowing the fisherman's own sensibilities to be released unharmed—but the fish themselves aren't always so lucky. They get eye-hooked, they bleed, they suffer trauma and dislocated maxillae and infection. Unavoidably, some die. For them, it is not a game, and certainly not a dance. On some days I feel that it's hypocritical to profess love for these creatures while endangering and abusing them so wantonly; better to enjoy the thrill of the sport honestly, kill what I catch, and stop fishing when I have had a surfeit of killing. On other days I do dearly enjoy holding them in the water, gentling them as they regain breath and balance and command of their muscles, then watching them swim away. The dilemma remains unresolved.

"Yet each man kills the thing he loves," wrote Oscar Wilde, and I keep wondering how a person of Wilde's urban and cerebral predilections knew so goddamn much about trout fishing.

Why do you live in Montana? people ask. For the trout, I answer. Oh, you're one of those fanatical fisherman types? Not so much anymore, I say. It's just a matter of knowing that they're here.

Early American Trout Fishing

Paul Schullery

Delegates to the Constitutional convention in Philadelphia some two hundred years ago were by all accounts made miserable by the heat. And I suspect that more than one of them must have daydreamed, as the proceedings droned on, of taking a shady seat by some stream in the countryside thereabouts, rigging up his tackle, and going in search of trout.

Imagine you were one of those delegates, or one of their assistants or servants. Once you realized there was no escape from the work of the summer—at least no escape that would give you time to do justice to a good trout stream for a few days—you may have sought some brief diversion in at least *getting ready* to fish. You may have done what so many do when they only have a little time to devote to fishing: *shop*. Philadelphia was a good place to do that. So you could have excused yourself, pleading some humble mission of personal comfort, and hurried from the hall and over to Market Street. There you delivered yourself and your daydreams into the hands of Edward Pole, "Fishing-Tackle-Maker."

Speaking as a historian who has his own idea of treasure, I would rather spend an hour in Pole's shop, with no money at all, than be turned loose with $1,000 in any modern tackle shop in the world. Established, as near as we know, in the early 1770s, he offered a full selection of gear to the avid anglers of southeastern Pennsylvania. He started advertising in *Dunlap's Pennsylvania Packet,* according to fishing historian Charles Goodspeed, in 1774, and by the year after the Declaration of Independence could boast an astonishing collection of stuff, the sort of list that makes modern tackle collectors dizzy with frustration that they cannot somehow be transported back there, buy one of everything, and bring it home.

The city-bound delegate could, judging from Pole's advertisements, waggle rods of cedar, hazel, or dogwood. He could crank "wheels" for trolling, bass fishing, or trout (these, like most of the other tackle, were usually imported), and could even get a first look at the new "multiplier" reels with gearing to speed up the retrieve of line (really now, is that sporting?). He could study the lines, "cable laid, from large dolphin down to whiting, with hooks suitable from Bonettar [bonito?] to the smallest size." He could rummage among the weights, swivels, snaphooks, and floats (cork). And of course he could lose himself in the fly display, examining and choosing among the "artificial flies, moths, and hackles" Pole kept on hand. If Pole was there he might engage him in conversation over the quality of imported horse hair versus the local variety (which Pole bought when he could, apparently to have lines made from it), or hear the latest gossip about Pole's competitors in the Philadelphia tackle trade (Pole, of course, announced he was better stocked "than any other in the city"), or ask him how business was at The Wigwam, Pole's tavern on the edge of town along the Schuylkill river, where fishermen were welcomed and coddled between outings astream.

Pole's expression may have darkened at this last question; things were not going well at The Wigwam, and in 1788 he sold out, the tackle business going to one George Lawton, who was still prospering in 1803 (and advertising an even greater selection of tackle; the lures included "Artificial Flies, Moths, Hackles, Minnew, Chubbs, Grafshoppers, Dilderries, Frogs, Mice, Birds, Cadds, &c. for Trout and other Fishing"), the year in which he sold a fair amount of durable tackle to the Lewis and Clark expedition. How long Lawton lasted we do not know, but Pole, Lawton, and their competitors are revealing by their very existence. They reveal the extent to which Americans enjoyed sport fishing long before they are believed to have.

American Angling Antiquity

We have been fishing for fun for a long, long time. Though fishing writers have often said that sport fishing in this country did not get a proper start until the 1830s, historical scholars agree that sport fishing, like many other forms of recreation, was popular as soon as the colonists found a little free time. Judging from the historical record, they found time early rather than late.

Carl Bridenbaugh, an important colonial historian, has noted that Collect Pond, later Freshwater Pond, in New Amsterdam, had by the 1630s become "the usual scene for open-air outings of fishing parties and 'unprofitable fowlers.'" In his *Cities in the Wilderness* (1938) Bridenbaugh pointed out that, by the time of the Declaration of Independence, Philadelphia's anglers had organized five different fishing clubs, the most famous being the first, the Schuylkill Fishing Company in 1732; no wonder Pole and his colleagues found good trade there. In her monograph *Colonial Virginians at Play* (1965), Jane Carson observed that "fishing was almost as popular as hunting, for food and for sport." In his fascinating *Angling in America* (1939), Goodspeed (who, while amassing great evidence to the contrary, did much to generate the myth that the colonists did not fish for fun) documented the fishing activities of many Massachusetts anglers in the 1700s, including several prominent citizens. By the early 1700s, residents of the many large and small communities in the colonies were known to enjoy hunting, fishing, skating, racing, and a variety of other traditional pastimes.

These first generations of sport fishers fascinate me. We know so little about the individuals. Fishing was not something to be written about then, much less published about. They left only incidental records—advertisements, journals, receipts, and the like (which is one reason fishing writers ignored their existence; most of our fishing writers have written fishing history as if it were merely the history of previous fishing writers). But they were fishing virgin waters, and think of the excitement in that.

I wonder, for example, about the Virginians, with their society so unlike Puritan Massachusetts; how many of those Virginian planters brought finely made tackle with them from the Old World?

And what of the earliest settlers of Pittsburgh, who have left diary accounts of the incredible richness of the fishery resources around their primitive fort? Who first dragged a fly rod along on that westward migration? Or, in the far left field of my historical wonderings, what of settlers of Spanish California? Thanks to the

11

research of Professor Richard Hoffmann, a Canadian medievalist, we know of *The Little Treatyse on Fishing* (1539), by Fernando Basurto, a fascinating fly fishing tract that establishes the extent to which Spanish sport fishing was based on a tradition independent of the British one. Did sport fishing find its way to the recreational interests of those first Euro-Californians?

These are not unanswerable questions. Sport fishing in the New World prior to 1800 is a wide open field, just waiting for the attention of more historians. The evidence will not be easily found, but it is there for those willing to do the work. Just recently I came upon a 1687 estate list, published in a Pennsylvania history journal, revealing among the property of James Harrison, master of Pennsbury Manor, "2 fishing Ceanes and a pasell of Lines." Whenever I see a mention of tackle like this (Ceanes are "canes," a term that was sometimes used even to describe higher-quality rods as well as "poles"), I wish I could know more: What did he fish for? What was his favorite bait? Did he frequent the trout streams, or stick with the warm ponds, or take pot-luck in the Delaware River itself?

Early American angling will for a long time cause those of us who care about fishing history to ask a lot of questions.

Trout Fishing Beginnings

Of course, we have no idea who first went out and caught a trout for fun, but it's clear that many people were doing so by the early 1700s. (It should also be remembered that many colonists found *subsistence* fishing and hunting something that was fun to do at times.) John Rowe (1757 to 1787), a prominent Boston businessman, kept a diary intermittently between 1764 and 1779 in which he occasionally mentioned his fishing (the diary's fishing entries were published with an introduction by John Phillips in 1929). He found excellent fishing in the ponds and brooks around Boston and Plymouth. On April 28, 1767, he fished at Duxbury Mills and "had very Good Sport, caught five Dozen Trout." The largest trout he mentions was eighteen inches, a substantial size for a stream brook trout in any age.

The earliest known fly fisher (though at any time an earlier reference may be discovered) in the New World was, appropriately, a British visitor, Joseph Banks, a young naturalist who visited Labrador and Newfoundland in 1766. Banks would eventually become a leading naturalist and President of the Royal Society but all that was before him on this trip, as he hoped to take enough specimens and do enough study to establish himself in science. Fishing historian David Ledlie recently

noticed in Banks's journals (not published until 1971) that the young scholar collected his fish specimens with flies. Banks, at one point, wrote that the trout he
caught in tidewater bit "particularly well at the artificial Particularly if it has gold
about it . . . ." Though the evidence is not incontrovertible, I have found probable
proof of a commercial fly *tier* in Philadelphia as early as 1773, when a Quaker
named David Hugh Davis was known to be making tackle at the George Inn.

What evidence we have indicates, not surprisingly, that trout fishing was practiced most often (at least as sport) near the settlements, out on the edges where
the fishing was still good. By 1800 trout fishing was well established in the
Boston–Cape Cod area, on Manhattan (Arch Brook, now entombed under pave-
ment and architecture, was once a fine brook trout stream) and Long Island,
in southeastern Pennsylvania (George Gibson, who would soon become one of
our first trout-fishing writers, started fishing the Letort and other Cumberland
County streams between 1790 and 1800), and presumably near other developed
areas with trout. It is not until just after the turn of the century, though, that the
historical record becomes easy enough to read for us to get to know many of these
fishermen personally.

The Rise of Trout-Fishing Society

Trout fishermen did not only become easier for *us* to identify in the years
between 1800 and 1860; they became easier for each other to see, too, and thus
created an important element of sporting society. The center of this movement,
this growth of self-awareness and communication, was sporting publication. Trout
fishing was by no means the subject of the largest part of sporting publications;
horse-related sports (known as "the turf"), hunting, dogs, and other topics got
more or as much attention. But trout fishermen did produce an impressive body of
material that had an enormous effect on the evolution of trout fishing in America.

These earliest trout-fishing journalists are not especially familiar to modern
readers. They have been unfairly ignored by most modern writers, who concentrate instead on the easy glamor of the later authorities and near-celebrities of fly
fishing—Theodore Gordon, Edward Hewitt, and so on. But our debt to these
early writers and thinkers is considerable. They have been neglected more out of
ignorance of what they did than from any conscious decision that they did nothing important.

Though occasionally a trout-related story appeared in the scientific or popular
press in the years between 1800 and 1829, it is in the latter year that we see a

major development, the appearance of our first sporting periodical. *The American Turf Register and Sporting Magazine*, established by John Skinner in Baltimore, was soon followed by the even more influential *The Spirit of the Times* in 1830. The *Spirit* was the work of William Trotter Porter, the most important figure in sporting writing before the Civil War and now universally recognized as the father of American sporting literature. Porter, through strength of personality and editorial skill, presided over the development of American sporting writing with an almost regal dignity and yet a fraternal warmth. He is one of the forgotten heroes of American trout fishing, partly because he chose to edit other writers rather than write books himself. But his guidance of others writers was wise and insightful, and he introduced American trout fishermen to practically all the major writers of the period, including British expatriate Frank Forester (the pen name of Henry William Herbert), certainly the most popular American writer on sporting subjects before 1890.

The Spirit and *The Turf Register* (Porter often edited both) were soon followed by other periodicals, many lasting only a few issues but all contributing to the flow of information and enthusiasm that characterizes sporting writing at any time. They accepted short reports and letters from correspondents in all parts of the country. When that didn't fill the necessary columns the editor himself would report on his own fishing. Or he would turn to the British journals, sometimes pirating shamelessly material that, with slight alteration, was made to appear American in origin, other times simply reprinting it with proper credit to the original British publication; American fishermen were kept well posted on developments in British fishing in this way.

It was an odd, not always easy to understand period in sport history, when Americans were torn between the traditions of their British forebears and the realities of American field and forest. The periodicals show a gradual transition from a near-total dependence on what had been learned on British trout streams to what we were learning on our own waters. Contrary to popular modern opinion, there is no one "birthplace" of American fishing, be it with fly, bait, or lure. There is only this uneven, ongoing (even today), and dynamic process by which we reexamine and redefine sports that we inherited from the Old World. Much of that process has taken place in the pages of our sporting press.

And, of course, the magazines were soon joined

by books. Some American fishermen were reading books by British writers, and soon were able to buy American books: J.V.C. Smith's *Natural History of the Fishes of Massachusetts* (1833), *Schreiner's Sporting Manual* (1841), John Brown's *American Angler's Guide* (1845) and his *Angler's Almanac* (1848 and later), Herbert's *Frank Forester's Fish and Fishing* (1851), and others, the number increasing dramatically after the Civil War.

Personalities and publishing history aside, what does this wealth of documentary evidence offer us, especially in answering that most important of questions, one we can ask across the generations almost as easily as we can ask it across a stream: "Whatcha catchin' 'em on?"

Practical Trout Fishing

The answer is pretty much the same as today: they were catchin' 'em on lots of things. They used flies (not always wet), they used lures (of a variety of materials including tin and wood), and they used bait of many kinds.

I could not begin to prove it, but I suspect that even as late as the Civil War the majority of American trout fishermen did not buy their rods. Unless they were fly fishing and had to take a little more care to get just the right action, they probably cut themselves an appropriate pole. Some of the best early American fishing books contained detailed instructions on how to build a good fishing rod. It was obviously much more a common practice in those days for a fisherman to build his own, even if he built a fairly fancy one, with "joints," "rings," and other hardware.

If they did not buy their rods, they probably used whatever sort of cord or line was at hand, and they probably didn't bother with a reel. We have received most of our knowledge of these trout fishermen from the few of them who wrote, and those few were among the most educated and best able to afford store-bought tackle. The mass of anonymous trout fishermen of 19th-century America will, like their counterparts in any previous century, probably remain anonymous.

But what of the others? What did you do, for example, if you were lucky enough to live near one of New York's several tackle dealers in the 1830s or 1840s, and if you could pay the price?

You probably were accustomed to the notion that one rod was good for any kind of trout fishing. You may have owned other rods—one for trolling for lake trout, one for saltwater, perhaps another for salmon if you *really* were flush—but most of your trout fishing, whether it was with bait or fly, was done with the same

15

rod. A good length would have been about 12 feet, maybe four sections, made of hickory or ash with the tip section of flexible, whippy lancewood. Such a rod would seem slow and floppy to a modern fisherman, but it had its advantages. It had a great reach for poking a short leader with a hooked worm into a tight corner of a brook, and it could throw a sweet, slow roll cast with a fly line. It was also, judging from the best surviving examples, extraordinarily handsome and a pleasure to hold. It might have been made either in England or America, but after 1850 there was no appreciable difference in the quality of the best rods from either country, and by then it may have been that our best reels were just a tad better than theirs; at least tackle shop promoters wanted to believe so.

In 1843, William Porter was honored by New York tackle maker John Conroy, who promoted "Porter's General rod," a model based on Porter's personal design. With this one Rod, Conroy claimed, you could do every kind of fishing. Through assembling the various alternative tips and other sections, it could become a light trout rod or a "heavy, powerful rod, sufficiently strong to play a thirty-pound salmon." It was apparently quite popular, though by the end of the century the idea of the general rod had lost all fashion and was even ridiculed.

Hooks were almost always attached to the line by a snell, the hook bound permanently to a short gut or hair leader. Snelled flies (the leader was tied onto the hook before the fly was tied) ruled fly fishing until well after 1900 in many parts of the country.

Baits were as they are: as numerous as the items in the trout's diet. Worms seem mentioned most of all, though minnows obviously were popular too. You used what you could get and, if the published reports are any indication, bait was all you really needed to catch a lot of trout.

There was no shortage of innovation and experimentation. Porter, writing about fishing in the Adirondacks in *The Turf Register* in September of 1840, described a rig for lake trout fishing that must have strained even his substantial creative resources:

> In trolling, we make our leader fourteen feet long, the precise length of our rod, using one of Conroy's patent reels containing three hundred feet of braided-silk line, strong enough to hold a 3 yr. old colt. At the end of our leader we had a set of snap-hooks, with a second set four feet above it, on each of which we played a live minnow, very much to our satisfaction, however they may have enjoyed it. Above the snaps at equal distances we looped on five large salmon flies. The

whole arrangement made something of a display, as we thought, and
the trout must also have been "mightily taken with it," for we took
two or three at a time.

Something of a display indeed! Even admitting that he was after 30-pound lake
trout, the gear seems a bit heavy, even if he was kidding about the three-year-old colt.

Flies were as much a matter of personal taste as they are now. Many of the early
authors (Forester and Brown among them) simply parroted the lists of flies in
British books, but some writers were already coming up with their own. General
George Gibson, a south Pennsylvania fly fisher whose fishing spanned the first
half of the century almost exactly, was developing his own patterns for the Letort
and Big Springs, when George Washington Bethune, in the notes to his important 1847 edition of Walton's *Compleat Angler*, made it clear that several of his
angling colleagues were experimenting not only with British patterns but with
their own variations and originals on waters from New Jersey to the Adirondacks.
American fly fishers were well on their way to developing their own approaches
to imitation by the end of the Civil War.

Pioneering New Waters

American trout fishermen seem always to have been wanderers. Even the first
exploring parties into some regions, such as the Lewis and Clark expedition, were
taking trout if only to eat or preserve as study specimens. But the vast American
wilderness beckoned irresistibly to generations of trout fishers, so irresistibly that
many waters were fished surprisingly early. Of course the coastal streams were
explored first, and those nearest inland settlements. But by the 1840s, sportsmen
had found their way into the immense Adirondack region and were already well
established along the shores of New England lakes and streams. A few recent
adventurers were reporting outstanding fishing in the Catskills and the Poconos,
and others were working their way farther west in Pennsylvania. A few fishermen
had discovered—and with unusual discretion not publicized—the monumental
trout of Maine's Rangeley region, and others were starting to fill in the many
gaps in the trout fishing map here and there: Vermont, Virginia, New York,
Pennsylvania, wherever trout waters could be found.

From those eastern outposts came the great leaps. By the 1850s reports were
coming in to the sporting periodicals of incredible trout fishing in California,
Oregon, and Washington.

In 1860 a naturalist, listing the fauna of Montana Territory in a scientific journal, commented incidentally that in that year soldiers were fishing for cutthroat trout in what would become the State of Montana, using both bait and flies. By ten years later even the exploration-resistant Yellowstone plateau had been fished with flies. A trout rod is not hard to carry and a few sharp hooks are a good hedge against hunger in the wild country; no wonder so many streams and lakes were fished so soon.

But the explorer and settler was often accompanied or preceded by the sportsman; sometimes all three were in one body. A man seeking a pass over a mountain range may also have been a husband seeking a cabin site or a trout enthusiast looking for a rise. It must have been enormously exciting, knowing one could find so many things at once: new country, a new home, unfished waters.

A central thesis of my book *American Fly Fishing: A History* is that it is to this rich variety of waters that we owe the remarkable diversity of our fishing tradition. Different waters, as several writers before me have noted, demand different tactics, so that sportsmen in each region, indeed on each stream and pond, are influenced by local conditions. It has been this collection of challenges that has brought us so much in the way of tackle evolution, new techniques, and even philosophical growth. For trout fishermen, like other sportsmen, are products of their environment. As we influence the trout and its world, so does that environment influence us. We are very lucky, in fact, that there *is* no single birthplace of our tradition; if there were it would be a far less vibrant tradition.

The Other Side of Trout Fishing

There is, of course, more to fishing than the tackle and the techniques, no matter how varied and colorful those may be. There is the complex intellectual baggage we carry along just as we carry our rods and our creels. There are the things we believe are right, or sporting, and there are the things we believe are important about the experience. It is this less tangible part of the trout fishing experience that explains why we read Robert Traver or Nick Lyons as avidly as we read Swisher and Richards or Art Flick. We long to know more about "how," yet we also want to know "why."

That is nothing new. Just as these early anglers debated which rods, flies, baits, and reels were best, they debated many other things. I find it especially apropos to modern trout fishing that they were like us in their prejudices. Listen to these voices from 150 years ago, and see if anything has changed. First, the grand old man himself, William Trotter Porter:

Fly fishing has been designated the royal and aristocratic branch of the angler's craft, and unquestionably it is the most difficult, the most elegant, and to men of taste, by myriads of degrees the most exciting and pleasant mode of angling.

Then try Chandler Gilman, from his book *Life on the Lakes* (1836):

Trolling! that vile, that murderous practice! abhorred at once and despised by all good men and true anglers. He permit it or countenance it? Never. The bones of old Izaack Walton would move in his coffin in horror at the degeneration of his disciple.

Then, from an 1832 correspondent from New Hampshire, writing to *The Turf Register* to complain that British flies were worthless for "catching Yankee trout":

I soon ascertained that the patent English line and *artificial fly* would not do. Our fish are too Republican, or too shrewd, or too stupid, to understand the *science of English* trout fishing. I therefore took the common hook and worm, with a simple line and light sinker, and a rod cut on the spot; they then understood, and we readily caught in a short time, twenty-three fine *brook Trout*.

These sort of gibes—some gentle, some mean, some deeply bigoted— appeared occasionally in the published conversations of anglers then as they do now. The process by which we define good sportsmanship is a never ending one. We will always differ with each other, to say nothing of with fishermen in other countries (however much we may lose touch with modern British fishing, we will probably never stop invoking Walton's name on behalf of our favorite argument), over what's right and proper in trout fishing. When it comes to a tolerance for the opinions and ideas of other fishermen, I can't say that we're all that much advanced over the trout fishermen of 150 years ago. But then, after all, we're only trout fishermen; what do I expect?

And yet after all my reading in early American trout fishing I find it immensely attractive. Like other fishing historians, including Ken Cameron and Austin Hogan, both of whom have commented on the desirability of being a fisherman in this period, I am attracted to those days. Knowing I cannot experience them is not a problem; I don't really want to. But at the same time I do want to understand them, to know what it was like.

I want to know not just so I can better understand how our sport evolved, though that does intrigue me, and not out of some arid antiquarian interest in old stuff (antiquarianism seems such a sterile pursuit, loving things just because they are old), but because fishing is a shared experience and I can share these great old fishing trips vicariously and quite pleasurably. What must it have been like, for example, to kill, as one *Turf Register* correspondent reported, 570 trout in one day on a Vermont stream, and to do so in a day when there was often no guilt attached to the activity? Well, according to the correspondent, it was sport better even than that "known to Izaak Walton of old, that prince of anglers; and such as few of us will ever have the opportunity of knowing again." True enough, if only because you can only do that to a stream once in a great while and still expect to find many trout in it again!

But there's no more point in resenting that foolish, greedy fisherman than there is in envying him; it's just that what he did is interesting to me. There is something to be shared in a fishing story, even if it's told in archaic language. It's the same thing we share when we read the modern books and magazines or swap tales with our friends. Trout fishermen have a sort of race memory in their written and oral traditions, so that they take great satisfaction in the accomplishments of earlier generations. We reread Gordon, Bergman, Wulff, and many others to repeat and share their triumphs and sorrows.

20   One thing that I have learned from studying our first trout fishers is that modern trout fishermen have, for all their talk of our grand trout-fishing tradition, let some of our best memories slip and be nearly lost. I suggest that we can revive and extend that memory, with good results, by researching, reading, and sharing the progress of several neglected generations of early American trout fishermen.

Blue Ridge Complex

Christopher Camuto

IF TROUT ROSE FREELY all year, there would be few fly fishermen. In the mountains, where rivers reflect the seasons as subtly as moving water reflects daylight, trout wait out the end of winter stirring, if they stir at all, in deep stillwater pockets out of sight. The fly fisherman, too, must wait while the year slowly straightens out under its own momentum, like a fly line during a backcast. There is in winter, as in other seasons, a critical pause during which a portion of the year unfolds.

The psyche of the fly fisherman is structured around important pauses—moments when something is about to happen—and a year in the field is mostly a matter of watching the edges of those moments carefully. Spring will emerge, in the guise of a mayfly or a black bear, when everything seems to stand still around a focal motion—a fluttering on the surface of a river, a sudden movement in the woods.

Although I know the fishing will be slow, I am drawn to the North Fork of the Moormans on warm February days when I sense the river might have slipped the season a degree or two. But despite slowly lengthening afternoons and the gradual browning of the gray mountains, the contracted mercury in my stream thermometer reflects winter's continued hold. The river is as likely to be colder as warmer from one trip to the next, but I dutifully chart its temperature from week to week: 38°, 37°, 39°, 37°. Until the water warms above forty degrees and stays there, I know I am going through the motions, fishing a cold shadow of last year's river.

On a given foray in early February I will nymph a familiar stretch of river for an hour or so, probing inside the cold, gray water for the edge of the season. On those brief winter afternoons I am, at best, remotely tethered to the river. My legs feel solid on its bottom, and the cork grip of the fly rod feels right in my hand, but from rod to line to leader, and then to tippet and fly, my senses diminish. At the fly, where a trout might be, I barely exist. In winter life in the river doesn't come to meet you, but I like to think as I wade upstream that each cast and well-mended drift brings trout toward me and urges the year on.

When I stop to change flies or tie on a fresh tippet, I find it hard not to watch those places where I know trout will be waiting in a month, eager to break the surface under an escaping mayfly. When sunlight filters through hemlock branches, brightening the flat slicks of slow water, I can't resist casting a dry fly. Even in February a Grizzly Wulff looks encouraging as it drifts at midpool or bobs on a standing wave in front of a boulder.

As I move upstream, I study the flow and structure of the river more carefully than I do at any other time of the year. I read its furrowed surface closely, as if each gray wrinkle in the current was a rune from a language by means of which rock and water and trout understood one another. Each boil and pillow and funnel of moving water is a sign worth noting. Possibilities circle slowly in each eddy. Had I not spent time trying to think through the signs on the water's surface to the remote whereabouts of winter trout, I would never have learned what the river looks like. I would never have noticed the miniature rivers within the river, the minute strands of finely structured current that have a life of their own and that represent the world to a trout. It was in winter I learned to take a trout's perspective and to see that a tiny spill of water over a cleft in a rock is far more significant than the picturesque cascade upstream that I might mistake for the center of the scene.

Whatever feel I have for unseen trout comes mainly from winter sessions of waiting, watching, and gently slip-striking barely perceptible differences in the dance of the line downstream to me. As I follow the line through a drift, I try to picture the nymph swimming toward a trout, wet body glistening with the tiny air bubbles trapped in the dubbed fur, long guard hairs feeling the current like legs. More often than not, I suspect, the fly moves unnaturally, dragged across conflicting currents by the leader or line, revealing my wooden presence.

A fly fisherman would be hard put to describe the subliminal difference between the slight shift of a line that has just been taken by a trout and the movement of a line that is being toyed with by a river. The life in a sine wave of current and the sinuous life in a trout are, after all, formed by the same forces. Each is an afterimage of the other. But compared to a trout, whose shocked particularity on the end of a line is unmistakable, the flow of a river is a generalization that, for all its subtlety, will never swim off the other way. So as the line comes toward me, I throw my vision a little out of focus and watch. Some differences seem animate and come to hand as trout. But these are sullen, dull fish—December trout—not the bright fish of a new season.

In midwinter I'm as likely to have a map as a trout in hand. United States Geological Survey maps hang on every wall of my study, some of the quadrangles a little ragged from their life in the field, creased wrong and burned here and there by cinders from campfires.

On Saturday mornings when rain or snow slants across the windows and hides the mountains from view, I haunt the map room at the University of Virginia's Alderman Library, laying out quads of places I haven't yet seen on the dark oak tables amid the detritus of snoozing undergraduates. Over the years I've pieced the Blue Ridge together in seven-and-a-half-minute chunks and searched the most promising rectangles for blue lines where clean, cold water might still filter through the crimson gill rakers of wild trout.

No doubt it is an accident of design, but the convoluted ribbing of contour lines on the topographic maps reminds me of the vermiculation on a brook trout's back and makes some important connections between land and trout clear. When I let a trout slip from my hand back into a river, I like to watch it lose itself slowly in the geometry of its habitat. The wormlike tracings on the olive back of a trout, refracted by the complicated play of daylight on the surface of a river, dissolve it in place. If a released fish doesn't dart away because of some sudden movement on my part, it will slowly transform itself under my gaze into something else—an algae-covered stone, a weed waving in the current, a shadow beside a rock.

The contour lines on the maps lead me back to the trout camouflaged in the landscape. Even in Alderman Library you can make some reasonable guesses about where topography suggests trout. Appealing blue lines follow the folded bases of ridges, descending through notches of closely spaced brown contour lines characteristic of the hollows and coves that structure the Blue Ridge. The size of a watershed gives me an idea of a stream's volume, and its gradient is a readable function of the spacing of the contours across which a blue line spills. Blue lines begin as bogs in saddles or springs in broken slopes, or simply from an accumulation of rainfall over a large enough area. The folds and slopes direct each blue line until it becomes a river and starts, in turn, to shape the land.

The thin blue lines are as vulnerable in the field as they look on the maps, each one a few precious miles of cold, flowing water and perhaps an enclave where wild trout thrive the way life tends to thrive on unexploited land.

There is only one way to find out.

Fish the blue line just after spring high water recedes, when the fishing is easiest. Get knee-deep in the line and wade upstream across the brown contours. Watch each shadow and weed and stone carefully, as if it might be a trout. Some blue lines pan out, surrendering wild trout to a fly. Others can no longer manage the transformation.

Although the modern USGS quads will lead me to the trout left in the mountains, the most interesting map hanging in my study is an old one, a reproduction of the Joshua Fry–Peter Jefferson map of 1751—"A Map of the Most Inhabited part of Virginia, containing the whole province of Maryland with part of Pensilvania, New Jersey and North Carolina." The Fry-Jefferson map was one of the first to show in fairly accurate if stylized detail the relationship between the country's rivers and mountains. The easternmost ridge is clearly labeled "The Blue Ridge," and it is possible that this widely used map settled the name of the mountains. For more than a century prior to this, settlers indiscriminately referred to the first blue line of mountains as the Blew Ledge, the Blue Ledges, the South Mountain, and the Blue mountains. Before rumors of the Rocky Mountains filtered east, some called the Blue Ridge the Great Mountains.

Although no one bothered much about the name of the mountains, almost every early explorer and commentator, as well as their Indian informants, mentioned the rivers to which they gave rise. In the late seventeenth century, John Bannister, the first trained naturalist in Virginia, summed up the importance of those rivers in terms as clear as the streams themselves: "If there be nothing that does so much conduce to the fertility of the soyle & wholesomeness of the air, & consequently to the health, profit, & pleasure of the Inhabitants: as clear running waters, & navigable rivers well stowed with fish: I know no country can boast of more or better than Virginia and Mary Land."

To me, the beauty of the Fry-Jefferson map is the detail with which it renders the free-flowing rivers that the country then boasted. The rivers on earlier maps tended to fade away uncertainly before they reached their source. The thin black lines on this map wend their way up into the mountains, as if the steep, cold head-waters were important. Some of the names have changed, and the map has its topographical inaccuracies, but many of the rivers I search for wild trout appeared there, drawn with some care, for the first time.

The past, of course, is another country, and neither modern nor old maps can take you back to what the mountains and the rivers once were like. Even in the field, it is hard to conjure up a useful sense of the past. One October several years ago I explored a stream that drops abruptly through the small gorge it has cut in the Blue Ridge escarpment near the Virginia–North Carolina border. I back-packed several miles down from the crest of the Blue Ridge through brilliant fall foliage, stopping to fish where the cascading water formed pools too irresistible to pass. I caught native brook trout in the upper reaches of the river, and then a mix of brook trout and handsome, streambred rainbows as I descended. By the time I stopped to camp, I was catching only rainbow trout, descendants no doubt of hatchery fish planted downstream.

I made camp and an early dinner, gathered wood, and then watched the river and the trout until dusk. When it got dark, I bundled up against the fall chill and built a fire. While I nursed the fire to life and felt the welcome heat and the famil-iar, mesmerizing effects of the flames, I tried to forget how close I was to the Blue Ridge Parkway on the ridge above and to a state highway not far downstream. I tried to forget that the watershed was a rare pocket of public land along a stretch of the Blue Ridge where very little land has been preserved for its own sake, and where few streams still supported a natural population of trout, brook trout or otherwise.

I stoked the fire until there was enough light to read by. I was reading a lot of history that year, trying to get an idea of what the Blue Ridge was like be-fore Indian trading paths became interstate highways. There is little mention of trout in the early exploration literature, but the mountains and the rivers are almost always in view. I had brought along a copy of William Byrd's *History of the Dividing Line Betwixt Virginia and North Carolina*.

The book read well in the field, perhaps because I was camped near the ground toward which Byrd and his surveying party had made their way in October of 1728. The land, of course, was nothing like what it had been in the early eigh-teenth century, but the wild trout in the stream beside me seemed proof of some connection that had not been completely broken.

William Byrd was more politician than poet, and far more of a land speculator than an explorer, but even his profit-seeking planter's eye was drawn, at times, into the beauty of the blue horizon toward which his surveyors blazed the line. And although fording and detouring around the innumerable streams that crossed his path was the principal labor of the journey, the clear-flowing rivers that led back into the mountains eventually eroded the edges of Byrd's materialism, freeing his imagination for short flights of appreciation of a landscape whose ultimate value, he seemed to discern, could be difficult to quantify.

Increasingly frequent halts to search out fords across rivers forced Byrd to look around. The closer he got to the mountains, the more he admired the bright, fast-flowing waters that tumbled from them. Temporarily stopped by dense cane-brakes along the upper Dan River, Byrd remarks on its extraordinary clarity. But when he thinks he sees something shining in the sunlit gravel of a broad riffle, his eye is dazzled by the old dream of gold that, two centuries after DeSoto's feverish march through the Southern Appalachians, still distorted the European view of the American landscape. "All our Fortunes were made," he remembers thinking. When closer inspection reveals the gold to be an illusion, Byrd is content to let the beauty of the river stand for its value: "However, tho' this did not make the River so rich as we cou'd wish, yet it made it exceedingly Beautiful."

Perhaps reading Byrd by firelight that night on Rock Castle Creek softened and distorted my view of him. Byrd's materialism and aristocratic hauteur are rarely far from view. But it seemed to me that by the time his men blazed a red oak beside Peters Creek to mark the end of the survey, Byrd had been, if not transformed, at least educated by what was then unspoiled wilderness.

I broke camp the next morning and backpacked and fished my way back to the crest of the Blue Ridge in what felt like bracing football weather. The small, quartz-studded gorge was beautiful and, if you followed the river, quite rugged in places. The streamside foliage was half shed, and as I worked my way upstream, shuttling the pack along, I found small trout holding under colorful pods of floating leaves. The trout leapt for any kind of small dry fly. When I found a thriving colony of rare walking fern, whose swordlike tips had traveled the length of a rock ledge that bordered the river, I got a sharp sense of a fragile, untouched world.

In a few miles I ran out of river and gorge and was back

on the Blue Ridge Parkway, where traffic broke the spell. The pristine wilderness that William Byrd and his cohorts approached in October of 1728 was gone beyond recovery, but there had been a tangy wildness in the crisp fall air and in the vivacious trout, as well as in the graceful presence of the walking ferns. Of course, Byrd was part of the vanguard of a culture that proved to be far from content with nature as they found it. Three centuries later, when the benefits and costs of that discontent have become apparent, only vestiges of wildness remain in the Blue Ridge—a few stands of virgin timber, some uninterrupted vistas, a remnant black bear population, some bobcat and timber rattlers, a few undisturbed habitats where rare flora and fauna persist, and the most subtle form that wildness takes—the quicksilver presence of wild trout.

As trout country the Blue Ridge is a Balkan affair. Trout survive where forested mountain land is preserved, where highland watersheds are left to function as their ecology dictates. Very little of the Blue Ridge is so preserved. You will no longer find wild trout everywhere in the Blue Ridge, but if you search them out, you will eventually come upon everything else of value in the mountains. Wild trout are a sign that the land is doing well.

I once asked a geologist friend in Asheville if the Blue Ridge could be defined. She smiled and showed me *her* maps. They bore less resemblance to mine than did the old Fry-Jefferson map. The maps on the walls of her office were geologic maps on which oddly shaped zones of dominant bedrock type were overlaid on the topographic features with which I was familiar. She pointed out what geologists call the Blue Ridge Complex, bands of ancient igneous and metamorphic crystalline rock that underlie the geographic Blue Ridge. I knew the basaltic greenstone belts in the northern Blue Ridge because my favorite rivers flowed over greenstone, and I knew to distinguish between granite and quartzite watersheds because the former weathered into a more mineral-rich riverbed. The rest of the puzzle was lost on me, and I was glad to hear that the closer geologists looked into the folded and faulted strata of the Blue Ridge, the less sure they were about how the pieces got together. *Terra incognita,* she called it.

My own Blue Ridge complex is a simpler affair, more a matter of personal geography shaped by two-hearted rivers, mountain trout streams that flow out of the past into the present, bringing wild trout with them. I have fished some of the classic trout water in the Catskills and New England. I have patiently worked the mesmerizing flows of the great spring creeks in central Pennsylvania, just north of the Blue Ridge. I have humbled myself on the big western rivers that have come to be the mainstream of the fly fishing world. I dream occasionally about fishing Alaska and New Zealand and all the exotic places you see on the covers of the fishing magazines, places that seem to get farther away each issue. Sometimes I imagine myself fishing for large brook trout in Labrador, on the Minippi or the Eagle, with a far wilder, far less compromised country around me.

But for the most part I've followed the blue lines into the Blue Ridge until the Blue Ridge became for me another country, a slender remnant of an almost lost world enveloped in a fading blue haze and filigreed in places with bright streams where wild trout come to a fly with pleasing frequency. Each year I have wandered a little farther north and a little farther south from the North Fork of the Moormans until I've gotten fairly far afield.

On the North Fork of the Moormans, the year lengthens upstream, pool by pool. During March, brief winter forays become long afternoons, half days paced slowly up the river from noon to dusk. The river comes alive in spurts, cascading ahead into spring and eddying back toward winter by turns. Warm days contend with cold ones, but even when the weather turns bitter, or a late snow throws the year on its back, the gray winter haze does not return. From a distance, the mountains are a warm, glowing brown.

In March everything is a sign: a stalked scarlet cup poking out of the leaf litter, a mourning cloak searching over a flowerless landscape, the white flash of a pileated woodpecker's wings clipping through the open woods. There are fresh beaver cuttings along the upper river. A half-dozen young sycamores lie felled aside one pool. Fresh toothmarks glisten in the soft heartwood of stumps around which are piled damp white shavings.

One by one fishermen appear like some strange species of wading bird that has migrated back to the river after wintering elsewhere. The same faces appear each year, in about the same sequence. They move slowly, fishing their favorite early-season reaches. Drowned and stillborn Quill Gordon duns appear in the seine, their wings crumpled around them. The early duns are small and very dark, almost black. The temperature of the river rises—39°, 41°, 40°, 42°—and the river seems to loosen and flow more freely. The days lose their finite, winter feel.

Trout must lose their dim consciousness of man during winter. They seem genuinely surprised each year by the predator who has learned to pretend he is part of the river, who seems to be both in and above the water, a little like a bear the way his form looms into the brightness over the river and the way his shadow darkens the riverbed, but a bear that can sting and tear at a jaw from a distance, invisibly applying a force that pulls with the threatening authority of the sky, a leverage that angles like nothing else in the river's current. The sensation is far stranger than the sudden grab of a raccoon from around a rock or the bewildering smash of a kingfisher from above.

Day by day my casting settles down. Eventually my wrist and forearm get a feel for the fulcrum between forecast and backcast where the line absorbs the energy of the rod and takes on a life of its own, quick and elaborately accurate. A long, light fly rod is a perfect tool on a small river. The long rod throws loops into the line and leader reminiscent of the curves in the current. The fly lights on the water out of nowhere, its graceful life in the air sustained by its drift on the surface of the river.

On a good day backcasts find space among the bare branches behind me, and the line flicks quietly forward into the cool air that flows over the river. It must be the alternate rhythm of wading and casting that makes fly fishing seem like searching. All day I am poised between the resistance of the river and the pulse of each cast, at the end of which a tippet unfurls and brings a fly to the water. Days tick forward with the rhythm of casting, held up only by the brief pause during which the line loads the rod.

29

Each year one trout in particular seems to start the year's fishing. This year I was a half mile below Big Branch, where the fire road is thirty feet or so above the river and long rays of mid-March sunlight slant into the water from downstream in the early afternoon, putting all the features of the streambed in sharp relief.

The trout held itself in the cold flow, its sleek green body quivering, tail to head it seemed, when it sighted waterborne prey approaching. I could see how it used its streamlined body to catch an edge of the current to move back and how it slipped the river with a twist to slide forward. Occasionally the fish would follow its prey downstream to the lip of the pool, taking the insect with a lunge just before fast water grabbed it. Then it would drop to the bottom, out of the flow, and return to its feeding position. Sometimes the trout responded to something in the current but did not take it, having made some final judgment against what it saw.

I was going to move on and leave this first rising trout of the year to feed in peace in that run between the boulders. But the weight of my fishing vest and the awkward feel of waders and heavy stream boots, as well as the fly rod in my hand, urged me down toward the river. And when I felt the sunlight on my face and neck and looked into the quick, sparkling water, I remembered the hand- and foot-numbing days of dead-drifting nymphs through slate-gray water I barely believed held trout.

I walked downstream fifty feet and worked my way down the embankment to the river. I approached the pool slowly, sidling along the near bank, trying to keep myself blanked against the trees. The riseform continued to pulse in place as I made my way into casting position.

I cast sidearm to keep the line out of the sky and managed to put a small Adams into the current above where the trout was holding, snaking enough slack into the line to get a good drift. I lost the fly in the glare but struck at the rise to which the drift was timed.

In hand, the first bright trout of the year always seems a bit unreal, almost abstract, as extravagant as a cockatoo. Taxonomically the brook trout is a char—a distinction without a difference to the fisherman—except that the word *char* has interesting roots, deriving obscurely from Gaelic and Welsh words for red, red-blooded, red-bellied. Whatever its lineage and taxonomic status, the Celtic etymology suits the bright, passionate fish. The scarlet spots on the flank of the trout, surrounded by their arctic blue aureoles, are the most exquisite detail in a landscape full of excellent design.

I fished through several more pools without success. Spring does not come on all of a sudden. The trout stayed hid, but I could not bring myself to go back to nymph fishing. I wanted winter behind me. The brown woods, bathed in sunlight, seemed to simmer with life, but a thin layer of cold air lay compressed over the river like a shadow stream, a winter soul.

I did not feel like starting back, so I hiked the fire road two miles to Tobacco House Hollow to see the head of the watershed and catch the end of the season. A winter chill clung to the mountains, but occasionally warm arms of air reached down the watershed from Via Gap. This was Shenandoah Valley air that, having simmered in the sun over freshly plowed fields, rose and flowed east through Blackrock Gap. As I walked I could feel spring pulling at the late-winter afternoon, feeling with long, intermittent breezes for a purchase on the year. The seasons seemed to be changing hands in the air overhead.

Where sunlight reached the river, I watched for trout. Occasionally I saw slender olive shapes holding in slow water and flashes of white when trout turned. Here and there rises bloomed on the surface of the river. At one point I stopped to watch a trout rising regularly, much like the one I caught. When the trout paused, I tried to make its slender olive form look like a stone, but I could not take the life out of it.

I sat and watched the river near an old homestead at Tobacco House Hollow. All around me signs of a vanished mountain culture were tangled in the understory—the remains of a school and a church and, farther upstream, the cemetery at the head of the river. With the sun off the water, the river went gray and looked cold again. Spring seemed to be losing its grip.

I thought about the people who used to live along the river. I wondered what lessons they taught at Via School and what prayers were prayed at the Wayside Church. And who was buried in that enviable spot at the head of the hollow near the source of the river? What had they thought about when they sat here, as they undoubtedly did, listening to the river, watching for trout, and waiting for spring?

As you come down the road from Via Hollow, you are far above the river for a mile or so. The watershed of the North Fork of the Moormans is laid out clearly before you. A large, exposed face of greenstone at the top of the Pasture Fence escarpment is the last feature in the landscape to catch the late-afternoon sunlight before the sun is lost behind the Blue Ridge. You can see it clearly at the top of the last steep rise in the road. For a few moments the rock face glows brightly, seeming to hold the sunlight in place. Then the greenstone darkens, and as you descend into the oncoming dusk the sound of the river rises as if to replace the waning light.

First Native

David James Duncan

ONE OF THE SIGNS OF A TRUE ARTIST, according to the Asian epic *Mahabharata*, is a willingness to work patiently and lovingly with even the most inferior materials. I mention this bit of lore in conjunction with the story of my first large native trout, because the fly rod with which I caught that trout was, essentially, a nine-foot-long opportunity to seek this sign of the artist in myself. The rod wasn't mine. Neither was I at the time. We both belonged to my dad, actually. But one day when I was about half the rod's length, the dad we both belonged to placed the rod in my hands, stood me on the banks of Oregon's Deschutes River, showed me the salmon flies crawling along the sedge grass and alder leaves, said, "Good luck," then thrashed off through a current too swift and deep for me to wade, out to an island, where he began to work the far riffle—

—leaving me utterly alone and utterly stunned, with this double-David-lengthed rod in my hand, this gigantic green river in front of me and this gigantic opportunity, the first in my life, to find out whether there was, according to the *Mahabharata*, any sign of the artist in me.

I didn't know, that day, that my fly rod was inferior. With nothing but a

stumpy green glass spinning rod to compare it with, I'd have been equally delighted with a Leonard, a Powell, or a pool cue. Which is lucky. Because a pool cue
is, basically, what my father had given me. It consisted of three yard-long, lumi-
nous, hexagonal lengths of Tonkin bamboo, the world's finest. The same bamboo,
after American B-52's turned the Tonkin Gulf into a moonscape, was worth its
weight in gold. My rod, however, was a pre-War effort: priceless raw material converted into a fishing instrument by Yankee craftsmen who'd taken the same degree
of care, and produced the same weight of implement, as the makers of some of our
finest garden hoes. Time and past owners had enhanced the rod further: it had
cracked and yellowed varnish, dark red wrappings on the guides that weren't elec-
trical-taped, black bloodstains on the hook-chewed cork handle and a most beautiful blue-green corrosion all over the reel seat. Its action brought to mind things like
spaghetti, wilted lettuce and impotence. The scrinchy, out-of-round reel and
antique braided flyline upped the weight total from hoe to shovel. But what did I
know? And, not knowing, what did I care? It is faith, not knowledge, that leads us
into paradise, and at age nine I had perfect faith that my reject rod, reel and line
were the most magnificent tools and the Deschutes the most magnificent river that
any sort of Dad & God combo could possibly have bequeathed me.

My paradise, though, had its raunchy edges. To pursue what needed pursuing
I had to step through a bunch of waxy-leafed vegetation that only retroactively
identified itself as poison oak. Then, like some nine-year-old prefiguration of a
contemporary fundamentalist homophobe, I had to catch this small, helpless male
homosexual salmon fly—or I assume it was male and homosexual, since it was
riding around on the back of its dead ringer, who in turn was riding the slightly
more voluptuous-looking back of what I took to be the female, since the probe-
thing coming off the middle male, the straight one, I guess you'd say, terminated
in her *fuselage,* I guess you could call it, and she seemed perfectly serene about
this. Anyhow, I nabbed the little humper up top, he seeming, in terms of the
future of his race, the least gainfully employed. Drafted him, you might say, which
makes me think: why would gays *want* to join the military? Because the instant I
drafted this guy I impaled him. No boot camp or nuthin'. Just impaled him, from
one end clear out the other, on a #10 barbed steel bait hook. No apology, no
prayer: that's where I was in terms of the spirit world. But the little trooper I'd
just skewered—think what you like about his sexual orientation—was about to
enact a Passion Play that I would never forget . . .

That he remained alive with my whole hook running through him didn't affect me at first. That his little legs kept kicking, and that the legs, or maybe they were arms, that weren't kicking started hugging my finger—even that didn't affect me much. But when I pulled his little arms off my finger, swung him out over the river, and he, seeing the wild waters below, suddenly opened multiple golden wings in the sunlight and tried, hook and all, to fly, he finally hit me where I live. And homophobe, hell, it was *way* worse than that: I felt like this nine-year-old Roman asshole who'd just crucified a little winged Christian. When he hit the water and, still fluttering, sank, a cold stone filled my throat. I have tried, however awkwardly, to pray for every creature I have knowingly killed since.

And yet—when I drifted my little winged Christian into a foam-flecked seam in the lee of my father's island, things happened that would very soon lead me to martyr many, many more such Christians. What can I say? We all live by sacrifice. As Tom McGuane once put it, "God created an impossible situation." But then salvaged it, I would add—or at least made the impossible lovable—by creating native trout.

For the first long instant of contact with my first great native, I saw nothing— just felt the sudden life pulsing, punching, shouting clean into the marrrow of my know-nothing, nine-year-old hands. But those little white hands, to keep feeling that wild electric pulse, suddenly forgot all about the things they did or did not know and began to work the ginked reel, dorked line and impossible rod with the passion and patience of some ancient craftsman straight out of the *Mahabharata*. Neither my hands, nor I, have been quite the same since. And when the fish, still invisible, turned from the quiet seam and shot into the white-watered heart of the river, my fly rod was never the same either: it was five inches shorter.

That native's first long run turned the whole hollow canyon and me into I don't know what—a oneness, music, a single-stringed guitar, maybe; and the way that blazing blue river played us, the sizzling song the line sang in the water, this alone would have indentured me to the Deschutes for life. But then my native revealed itself—the rainbow, the whole shining body flying up out of the water, filling me for the first time, then again and again, with so much yearning and shock and recognition and joy that I can no longer swear I remained in my body.

Every fisherman knows the basic alchemy: you place an offering on a steel point; you throw it in the river; your offering sinks despite the beating of its wings; you feel terrible, yet dare to hope a miracle will take place; then one does: the river converts your meager offering into an unseen power that enters your whole body

35

through your hands. An old metal reel you mistook for tackle starts to shriek like a wounded animal. Your old rod breaks but keeps lunging. Your heart does the same. Then, with no wings at all, native life comes flying up out of the river—and that's when a hook's point pierces *you*. A barbed point, you realize later, because even when the day ends, the change in you does not. By the time you hold the native in your hands it is you who has been caught; you who shines, and feels like silver; you who came, long ago, from water; you who suddenly can't live without this beautiful river.

Walk on Water for Me

Lorian Hemingway

I TAKE FISH PERSONALLY, the way I have my life, like a sacrament. This is my body. Eat of it. This is my blood. Drink. I imagine this reverence is what they want of me. The alchemists made an eyewash (collyrium) of fish, believing it would bring omniscience. I've tried to envision the process: cooking the fish, as the alchemists instructed, until it "yellowed," mashing it into a crumbly pulp, mixing it with water and then filling the eyes with this paste so one might gaze with as much dimension as trout in a clear stream. But as with all things in alchemy it was the process that mattered, the final result never as important as the ritual preceding it.

Knowing fish is a process. I have been acquainting myself for forty years. To know fish you have to have been intimate, the way the alchemists were. The first fish I ever caught was a baby bass netted from a deep Mississippi ravine I lived near during summer. It was my refuge, that ravine, a place of discovery, revealer of miracles, its depth filled with a heavy current of reddish-brown water during the spring floods, its clay bottom dried to a pockmarking of deep holes by mid-July. I was tirelessly curious when I was young, bound inextricably to all natural mysteries beyond four walls, nervous and jumpy if made to sit too long indoors, recalcitrant once sprung. I'd watched this particular fish for days, trapped in a pothole in the ravine, swimming in a quick panic from one side to the other, instinctively seeking a tributary leading from its footwide prison. I empathized, imagined myself locked in my room for days, dizzy and breathless from ensuing claustrophobia, frantic enough to pull up the flooring with my bare hands. I understood feeling trapped, my life then nothing more than a crash course in how to escape.

After a few days the water in the pothole had diminished by half and grew so thick with ravine mud that the fish hung motionless in the ooze, its gills laboring for the oxygen it needed. On my knees I stared into the hole, goldfish net in hand, thinking it was evil what I was about to do, snatch a living creature from its habitat and bring it, luckless, into my own. I remember the delicate, thin striping on its flanks as I lifted it, unprotesting, from the muck, and how soft and filmy the skin felt as I stroked a finger along his length. I remember, too, how my heart raced as I dropped the fish into a jar, watched him sink quickly and then just as quickly take his first breath in a new world. Within moments he was moving through the jar as manically as he had the pothole days before. I had given resurrection in a pint of water, become God to a fish. Years later I would remember that moment as one of grace.

Fish became my fascination, and began to appear in dreams, their shadows deep in dark water, cruising, fins breaking the surface from time to time, a teasing swirl of movement as I stood on shore with net or rod or hands poised to strike. In one dream I stood before a pool of monster fish with bare hands greedy, my fingertips singing the way a line does when it's pulled free from the spool. As I leaned forward, a shape would slide deliberately beneath my reach, and I would lunge into water that was dense and thick as oil, only to come up soaked and empty-handed.

I don't know now that the dreams had to do with catching fish, but rather with some unconscious, archetypal need. I have consulted Jung on this one for the obvious, loaded symbolism. I have even dreamt, in these later years, of Jung, standing atop the stone fortress of his tower at Bollingen, fly rod in hand, a wooden piscatorial carving dangling from his leader line. He smiles in the dream, proud of himself. He did say water is the unconscious and that fish are a Christ symbol. I deduce then, from these two boldly fitting pieces, that I am at times fishing for Jesus, or in some way, in recent dreams, dry-flying for Christ. I like the simplicity of it, the directness. I like that it speaks to Christian and Hedon alike.

But during those Mississippi summers I paid little attention to dreams, mes-merized then by a world filled with fish, snakes, turtles, toads, and lizards, any-thing remotely amphibian. I progressed from netting bass to catfishing with a bob-ber and worm, frittering away entire days on the banks of muddy lakes, certain, always, that the fish lived dead center in the middle of the lake, assuming the notion that the truly elusive spend their time where we can never hope to reach them. To cast where they hid became my ambition, and once mastered I under-stood that fish went wherever they damned well pleased, unimpressed by my clumsy form hurling hooks into their midst, immune to my need to know them.

I had patience, the sort I suspect God has with people like me. It was nothing to be skunked for days on end. I lived in perpetual hope of seeing that wayward shimmy of the bobber, then the quick dip and tug that signaled I had made con-tact with aliens. At that time in my life this was my social interaction. I talked to the fish hidden deep in the ponds and streams I visited, trying to imagine what they saw beneath those mirrored surfaces and reasoned it was hunger and not stu-pidity that made them take bait so crudely hitched to an obvious weapon. Compassion surfaced. I pictured scores of starving fish grubbing for worms only to be duped into death by my slipshod cunning. When I'd reel them to shore I'd cry at what I'd done, at the sight of the hook swallowed to the hilt, at the flat, accusing eyes of the fish, and then I'd club them with a Coke bottle, the heavy green kind with the bottling company's name on the bottom. No one ever said there was another way to do it. In Mississippi, there was the hook, the worm and the bobber, a holy trinity on a hot day in August—low-maintenance fishing I call it now. My guilt was usually pushed aside by their quick death beneath the bot-tle, and eating what I had caught seemed to remove the shame considerably.

My favorite fishing hole—I look back on it now as Mississippi's version of Mecca—was a place that to this day I am certain only one other knew of, the landowner who'd barbwired it off and posted a huge, hand-painted sign along the fence—Warning: SNAKES. Roaming deep in a pine woods in rural Hinds County one summer afternoon, I came upon the pond, the edges of it rising in volcanic fashion from the otherwise flat land. I was accustomed only to ponds that were slipped like sinkholes into the surrounding pastureland, and as I made my way up the slight incline of earth, hands grasping the barbwire delicately, I beheld, not a rock quarry as I had expected, but instead a perfectly black pool of water, its dimensions no greater than those of an average swimming pool. At first I could not believe the color of the fish who were pushing to the surface, dozens of them, nosing one into another, their bodies as opalescent as pearls, and huge, their lengths dissolving into the shadow of the pond. I had never seen albino catfish, had never seen *any* white fish, and thought for a brief, illogical moment that they had been segregated from their darker mates simply because of their color. In Mississippi, then, it fit.

To have called this pond a fishing hole is misleading. I never actually fished its waters, too mesmerized by the cloudlike shapes that moved without sound through the deep pond, believing, beyond all fishing reason, that to catch them would bring the worst sort of luck. So I watched, alone in the woods with these mutants, some days prodding their lazy bodies with a hickory stick, which they rubbed against curiously, and on others merely counting the number of laps they made around the pond in an afternoon, hypnotized by the rhythm they made tracing one circle upon another.

The fish were as truly alien as my starkest imaginings, and I became convinced they were telepathic, reading my thoughts with such ease I had no need to speak to them. I called these sojourns "visiting the fish gods," my treks to that mysterious water that had no business existing in dry woods, and took into adulthood the memory of them, as if they were a talisman, granting me privileges and luck in the fishing world others could only dream of.

As I grew older I began to think of fish as mine. I'd been in close touch with them long enough to develop something that I believed went beyond rapport and came, in time, to border on feudalism. Fishing became far more than sport or communion. It began to develop the distinct earmarkings of a life's goal. No longer content to watch and prod, no longer in command of patience, I lived to fish, becoming, in my own mind, a fishing czarina, my luck with rod, reel and bait phenomenal.

Self-taught in the simple mechanisms of spinning gear, I had perfected a bizarre way of holding the reel and rod upside down while casting and retrieving. It is something I have never been able to undo, the habit of flipping the rod over before I cast worn into my nerve pathways like my image of Christ as a skinny Caucasian. Years later someone told me I cast like a child. So what. It never marred my accuracy, and in fact I was a little pleased childhood habits had stalked me this far. I was also told "any idiot can catch fish with a dead piece of flesh and a bent nail." I *was* an idiot, but smug in my idiocy, refusing to let go of sure-fire methods I'd known as a kid in Mississippi. Holding true to my fundamentalist, country fishing ways, I began to gain a reputation for being the only person certain, on an out-ing, to catch fish. An attitude surfaced as rapidly as fish to my bait. Men were forced to regard me now, but warily, as I moved within their circles, trying always to outdo them. Gone was the solitary fishing of my childhood, the secret visits with fish gods. I had become competitive.

I cannot place the exact time when my fishing innocence turned streetwalker tough, when imagined power over the waters of childhood turned to a calculating game, but I suspect it was when I discovered that good-old-boy fishing and beer went hand-in-hand. I'd been drinking plenty before I became truly obsessed with bait and tackle, but now I began articles I wrote on the subject with lines like "Nothing like a cold six-pack in the morning," causing my editors to wince and accuse me of writing manuscripts "afloat in beer."

I took to drinking the way I had to that ravine in summer, daily, and the false tough-girl attitude it fostered launched me into an arena that included the truly elusive, monsters who swim leagues deep in saltwater. Armed with the fishing world's equivalent of an elephant gun, I hunted tropical waters for marlin, shark, tuna, tarpon and barracuda, catching them all, tearing muscles and breaking blood vessels while in battle, but anesthetized to the pain because my six-pack in the morning had now become a full case in a five-hour stint.

The popular image of a fisherman sitting on the bank on a quiet Sunday afternoon, pole propped against a rock, cold beer in hand, contemplating, was about as close to what I did on the water as Andy Warhol is to Degas. On board I was a one-armed windmill in one-hundred-knot winds, my hand dipping in the cooler for a drink as fast as I hauled fish on deck. I was Macho Woman. Back off. This is the life, I told myself a lot during those days, the idea that one occasionally encounters periods of grace eluding me entirely.

Still, I was ashamed when my prey would slide alongside the boat, exhausted, beaten to near death. I'd release them, guiltily, my hand still reaching involuntarily for the Coke bottle, now a flimsy aluminum can, worthless as it turned out, for any feat of strength. People would slap me on the back and say things like, "You fish like a man. You drink like a man," offerings that in the light of what I was to become seem almost comical now. But at the time I considered it an honor, posing willingly with other people's four-hundred-pound slabs of dead marlin, beer can held aloft, grinning crookedly, a mutant now compared to that girl bent over the potholes, goldfish net in hand.

For several years I was flat-out on the gonzo stage of fishing, where any method of felling fish was acceptable. I never batted an eye at ten-pound teasers rigged to the transoms of forty-foot sportsfishermen. The anchor-sized saltwater reels looked normal to me, and fifty-pound test, what the hell. I had lost sight of that first delicate intimacy, the tiny bass swimming clearly in my see-through jar of river water. I no longer practiced communion, but sacrilege. My life, as well as my fishing, had turned brutal.

I prefer the confessional to the cross, figuring if I own to enough treachery I will be spared in a moment of mercy, like that bass in the ravine. When I quit drinking—finally—after an eight-year period of uncommon buoyancy on sea as well as land, my liver shot, my eyes as yellowed as the fish the alchemists sought for insight—I quit the gonzo lifestyle. "Blind drunk" is not a phrase without meaning, and to me it came to mean that I had been blind, almost irrevocably, not only to the damage leveled in my own life, but to the life beneath those waters that came so frequently in dreams.

Dead cold sober now, I took up fly fishing. Not on the same day, certainly, because the shakes wrack you for a while and all you're really good for is mixing paint. I'd held a fly rod only once during my fish killing days, off the coast of Islamorada during tarpon season, while fishing with legendary guide Jimmie Allbright. In the saltwater fishing world, *guides* and *anglers* are legendary, never the fish who serve them. After meeting enough of the old masters, I came to the conclusion that to become legendary all one needed was to catch oversized fish and not die from sunstroke or lip cancer, tie a few exotic-looking flies, cast phenomenal distances against the wind and remain steadfastly laconic when a novice is on board. What I remember most of the first fly-fishing experience is a lot of yeps and nopes directed at my questions, the fly line cinched tightly around my ankles after a bad cast, and a sunburn that bubbled the skin on the tops of my ears. It was a waste of energy, I figured. I didn't get the point. All that whipping and hauling and peering into the distance just reminded me of bad Westerns.

But something happens when you get purified, take the cure, lob your body onto another plane of perception. Without a beer in hand fly fishing seemed far more appealing to me than it had when I'd been trolling with bait big enough to eat. Back then I'd called it effete, elitist, prissy, egg-sucking. I figured the entire state of Montana was crawling with seven million people who looked exactly like Robert Redford, all of them hefting custom fly rods. Now in a completely altered state of mind, I began to notice the grace involved in a simple cast, how the arm of a good angler was merely an extension of the fly rod. I studied the art a little, secretly, not yet ready to be labeled a wimp.

About the time I was reading Izaak Walton's *The Compleat Angler,* I got a call from Florida writer and fly fishing guide Randy Wayne White asking me to fly fish on his PBS-syndicated fishing show, "On The Water." I didn't tell the man I couldn't cast spare change into the hand of a willing Hare Krishna, much less fly cast for tarpon, which was what he had in mind.

"Sure," I told him, eager, as always, for a new opportunity to humiliate myself. "I've caught tarpon before," neglecting to mention it was with an orange Day-Glo bobber and a live mullet. I wanted to be prepared and figured with all I'd read on the subject I could learn the basics in half an hour of hands-on practice. So after taking a quick lesson in a downtown Seattle park, I flew south.

I was soon sitting anchored off a mangrove island on Florida's west coast with Randy. Randy Wayne White is what you would call a burly man, built like a fireplug with forearms the girth of oak saplings, an image that belies his physical grace, and particularly his ability with a fly rod.

"Where'd you learn to cast, Lorian?" he was asking politely as he grinned into the sun and the PBS camera, while I whizzed a live pilchard past his head. He hadn't seen me fly cast yet because I'd begged off after watching Randy sail his line eighty feet toward a school of feeding redfish. Nah, I'd told myself after watching a redfish pounce the fly, this won't do. I was out of my element entirely, beerless, baitless, naked.

"I never did learn," I told him, my back to the camera as I slung another pilchard into the mangroves. "Amazing, isn't it," I said, "what you can teach yourself." Randy nodded, his eyes losing hope. This exchange never survived the edited version of the show's tape, and in subsequent shots the camera gently panned away into the mangroves, or to the pelicans flying above, as I cast upside down and reeled backwards, dragging whole mangrove tubers boatside.

The second day out we headed in Randy's flats boat for the coast of Boca Grande where scores of tarpon were rolling on the surface of the water. Randy slapped a custom, saltwater fly rod into my hand and said, "Go for it, Lorian!"

Go for what? I remember thinking. For what, for Christ's sake. It was enough in a ten-foot chop on a three-foot-wide boat to merely right myself and stand there lurching starboard, portside, fore and aft, like one of those sand-weighted plastic clowns that lean wa-ay over but never quite go down. I viewed the wallowing tarpon at eye level and imagined offering my lunch as chum into the churning water.

43

"There're hundreds of them, Lorian. Hundreds. Go ahead and cast," Randy called from the stern.

I think I pulled maybe six inches of line from the reel before I noticed the particular leaden quality of the sky just north, south, east and west of us, as Randy yelled, "Two o'clock. Tarpon at two o'clock."

The sky at two o'clock looked like midnight with the occasional atomically bright lightning bolt shearing the blackness.

I'm no fan of lightning while in an open boat, no fan of lightning while wearing a rubber suit in a six-foot-deep cellar. It's a phobia of mine—call it silly—one that's rampant, unchecked, paralyzing.

"Graphite," my head said. "You're holding a goddamned graphite rod." PUT IT DOWN. What they don't tell you about fly rods is that they're superb electrical conductors, right up there with copper. I chucked the rod in Randy's direction, hit the deck and yelled "Drive!" about the time a bolt struck dead center off the bow and the air turned crispy crackly with electricity. I could feel the hair on my neck and arms rise up.

I spent the beat-your-kidneys-to-Jello ride back to shore face down in the boat, my nails tearing at Randy's left calf, hissing Hail Marys, as lightning popped in the water around us.

"Next time I see you, I'll give you a casting lesson," Randy told me the next day, as I wandered around randomly kissing the ground, his hand, the cheeks of strangers, stunned to be alive.

"Like fun," I said.

It took a while before I could look at a fly rod again without itching to buy life insurance. But the dreams returned, this time of pink speckled trout in blue streams, less threatening than tarpon in boiling, black water, and I thought, sure, that's where I belong, in a trout stream wearing waders and a nifty fly vest displaying hand-tied flies, maybe a telescoping depth wand strapped at my hip, Swiss army knife dangling from that ring on the vest pocket. That's me all right, the Orvis girl. And since I figured you don't have to be a ballerina to dance, I took up casting again, practicing in my back yard—and a one and a two—secretive and clumsy, the cat my only witness. Somewhere around my fortieth birthday my husband Jeff had given me a new rod and reel, complete with weight-forward line, and I took to the business of learning to cast as earnestly as I take to anything, which means if I don't master it on the second or third try, I quit, stick out my lower lip and glare.

I had achieved mid-beginner status (capable of placing the fly on the water by wadding the line in my fist and heaving it) when Jeff and I took a trip to the Salmon River in Idaho. I had taken fish there years before, six-pack in hand, spinning gear in the other, dragging the rocks—twenty-four trout in half a day, my finest hour, but drunk when I did it so maybe the count's off by half. I wanted to return to make amends, to take a trout clean and easy without the heavy artillery.

The Salmon is a beautiful stretch of water, clear, relatively shallow and fast, unlike the slow, clay-weighted waters of Mississippi. When I first moved to the Northwest I was amazed you could see so deeply into the water and would sit for hours on a river shore staring at the rocks beneath. Jeff, on the other hand, grew up with this purity, which may explain why it seems to be in his blood to fish these waters, and fish them well, in fact better than anyone has a right to. He has the sort of luck with a fly rod that I used to have with bait, a fact that has compelled me to accuse him of actually robbing me of fish-luck, a high crime in our marriage.

Our first day on the river I'd waded in bare-legged and was fishing generally the same area of water as Jeff, but politely upstream so the fish would get to me first, when his luck (he calls it skill) kicked in. He'd released six fish before I'd even gotten my fly damp. Normally I handled such flagrant displays with stoicism, wanting to keep my image as a good sport intact, but this day was different. I'd returned to waters that had blessed me once with uncanny luck, to waters that had kindly not swallowed me whole as I'd staggered through them, and all I wanted was that brief, immortal contact with aliens, the way I'd known it when I was a kid, new and simple. I was obsessed that day with taking a fish on fly. I'd read A.J. and Norman. I'd gone to the outdoor shows. Nothing seemed more perfect or vital than the feel of a trout on the end of that nerve-sensitive line. I'd felt how mere water current could electrify the line, transforming it to a buzzing high-voltage wire, and I wanted some of that magic.

"Yee—ha!" Jeff yelled from down river as he released another perfect form into the water.

I false cast and hooked my chin.

I could feel them all around me, the sense of them, fish moving the current in swirls around my bare ankles, fish swimming between my thighs. I inched my way in Jeff's direction, watching his fly line thread out before him and then drop like a whisper onto the water.

I got within twenty feet of the man and flung my line in an awkward sidecast right where I'd seen his last fish surface. I waited. I prayed. I watched. I peered.

Nothing.

My husband is someone who takes athletic grace for granted, figuring it's something we all can achieve in time.

"Your presentation's wrong," he told me.

Had I read about this? I searched my memory.

"My what," I said, coming up blank.

"The way you're putting the fly down. It's wrong."

Well, what the hell. It was enough, I thought, to get the fly in the water. Who could resist after that. And when did fish get so picky, worrying about presentation, the particular color of a hackle. With worms there had been no guesswork. Eat this tasty sucker, you cretin, I was thinking as I fingered a rubber worm I'd stashed in my vest pocket.

"Fish are color-blind," I said with some authority, apropos of nothing.

"So," he said in that way he has that tells me he's already written a book about it.

To illustrate presentation, Jeff whipped off another perfect cast. A trout rose to his fly, and bingo, the water around us was alive. I hated him.

"Maybe it's my fly," I said.

I waded over to him and switched rods, thinking, *Okay you, give me that magic wand, we'll see who catches fish.*

"Yours casts so easily," he said as he set the line in motion.

Wham. I swear to God that fish hit the fly in mid-air.

"Nothing's wrong with your fly," he told me as he released the biggest trout of the day.

"That's it," I said, stomping toward shore as gracefully as possible in four feet of water. I'd snatched my rod from him and threw it on the bank when I emerged, soaked and cold, as pissed as I'd ever been.

"I thought you were a good sport," I heard him calling from the river.

There, I'd blown it. Years of cultivating an image, gone.

"Go to hell," I yelled. "Go straight to hell, you and your stupid fly rod, you jinx. Jinx! Ever since I've fished with you I've caught nothing. Not a goddamned thing. You took all my luck, and now you rub my nose in it. I'll never fish with you again. I swear to God."

I sat down on the bank and literally stomped my feet, hands clenched into fists at my sides, my heartbeat clearly audible in my temples. I'd heard about people like me. Poor sports. Whiners. Lunatics.

"It's just your technique." The wind carried his words so that "technique" seemed to be underlined, and I shouted back, "Eat your technique. Eat it, you hear!"—a response I thought fair at the time.

It was then I saw the naked man in the raft drifting past, fly rod poised in mid-air. Ordinarily, naked would have been enough, but as I watched more closely I noticed he was throwing his rod tip up to twelve o'clock and then waiting for a beat before following through with the forward cast. During that beat the line straightened out behind him, unfurling slowly from the arc it made as he brought the rod forward. Again he cast, my own personal naked instructor, oblivious to me on the bank, and again with the same hesitation. Some technique, I thought, peering in Jeff's direction to see if he'd noticed the man. Nah. Naked women could have been skydiving into a bull's-eye on his head and he'd have kept on casting. I watched the man cast another perfect length of line and discovered my arm moving involuntarily, following his motions. I watched his wrist. Hardly a bend in it as he pointed the rod arrow-straight in the direction of the unfurling line. At that moment something settled into place, the way it did that one time I bowled a strike, and I saw the whole process, not as frantic thrashing and whipping, but as one liquid motion, seamless and intact. It was the way, I thought, I should have always fished, naked, tethered to the water by a floating umbilicus, aware.

I spent the rest of the day practicing on a dirt back road, heaving that line at first as if it were a shotput. When it would drop in a dead puddle at the end of my rod I'd try again, remembering the vision of that man in the raft, his perfect rhythm, the way he seemed to notice nothing but his line as it spun out above the water. I kept trying against what I considered rather hefty odds until I had my line singing in the air and pulling out the slack around my feet as if it were ribbon shot from a rifle. I grew calm from the effort, a way I'd not remembered being for years. I looked at my hands, steady as rocks, as they rose above my head, left hand experimenting with a double haul. Hey, I thought, I might get good at this.

That evening at dusk I caught my first fish on a fly, a beauty I watched rise in a quick thrash, greedily, as if he'd been waiting all day for my one ratty fly, frayed and battered from the day's practice, but oddly noble. It's all I wanted, that one fish, electric on the end of my line, and, God, how I could feel him, his jumpy on-and-off current carrying all the way up my arm. How do you do, I felt like saying, it's been a long time. I wet my hand and cradled his girth in my palm. Such a nice feeling. Moist, alive, not slimy the way we're taught to think. I pulled some water through his gills and released the fly from his lip, delicately, no sweat, and watched as he fluttered and then dove in a quick zigzag, deep into the stream. For an

47

instant I remembered the delicate feel of the baby bass as I slopped him into the jar of river water, then the fish gods, white and huge, circling the perimeter of the pond, aware, perhaps, of nothing more than the rhythm their movement created, and in that instant, I too, here in the clear water of an Idaho stream, understood rhythm, but as if it were the steady beat of childhood fascination returned.

In my new dream there is the same dark pool from childhood but its expanse reaches from the very tip of my feet to the horizon in all directions, its surface flat as undisturbed bathwater, the shapes beneath it perfectly formed now, truly fish-like and sharply defined, the tails like so many Geisha fans slapping left and then right in unison, a metronomic rhythm setting forth visible currents beneath the water that never break the calm glassiness above. I marvel at the dance, watch the fish line up, nose to tail, in a perfect circle, swimming faster and faster. I look to my empty hands and realize my husband stands to my left ready to make a cast with my new white lightning rod. I say, "Give it to me. Now," and cast a Royal Coachman out to Jesus. "Come on boy," I call across the pool, "walk on water for me." The fly taps the skin of the water, and the circle of fish shatters like beads in a kaleidoscope, bathing me in light.

The Novitiate's Tale

Marjorie Sandor

AT THE SOUTH END OF DARBY, Montana, right before the speed limit goes up and the Bitterroot River comes back into view, there's a Sinclair station with a marquee that looms like wish-fulfillment: all in capital letters, like the message DRINK ME on the little bottle Alice finds, this marquee reads: DIESEL, UNLEADED, FLIES.

What is it about the prospect of trout-fishing that turns the novitiate's simplest act—that of buying a couple of flies or a new leader—into a quest, a rite of passage? There was a long riffle just upstream from Darby that looked magical to me—it had to be full of rainbows—and waiting through a week of work to get there, I hungered for it as unrequitedly as I do for certain film stars and countries I'll never get to: secretly, with idiotic surges of adolescent chills-and-fever.

Practically speaking, I needed a leader. I strode to the screen-door of the Sinclair station, heavily booted like any hero, but faintly aware of my relatively small size and deep ignorance. The whole business seemed a dazzling path to certain failure: wrong fly, too hot a day, too cold, wrong spot, wrong way to fish right spot—infinite and thrilling were the ways.

In a small room beyond Wheat Thins and Jim's World-Famous Jerky, a man waited behind a glass case of flies, reading the newspaper with the tricky nonchalance of all guardians of the dream world. A few packets of hooks and spools of fishing line hung on a pegboard. The whole thing looked preposterously spare and anti-mysterious, like a false front.

The man smiled when I asked for a tapered leader. "Just startin' out, are we?" he said. "You don't need it. You'll do fine with plain old monofilament." And he brought down a spool of what looked to me like purple sewing thread.

"I'd really prefer tapered leader," I said, in the hushed, careful voice of someone asking for groceries in a foreign country. He, in his turn, waved his hand casually in the air, as if my remark were utterly irrelevant.

As I took the monofilament and two locally tied nymphs, he followed me out and told me not to go to that dumb fishing access point—the place'd be crawling with tourists. He drew a spidery, complicated map of a secret hole *no out-of-towners know about,* which I could only get to by trespassing on a local rancher's property. "He doesn't mind," he said, and tipped his hat. As he followed me to the screen-door he added, with a dreamy air, "You'll learn the hard way on that monofilament. Believe me, when you get back to tapered leader, it'll seem like a breeze."

Suffice it to say that though I fished the wrong spot all day, with the wrong line and the wrong fly, the Bitterroot itself, with its willow-shaded margins and islands, its riffles and runs and promising boulders all just out of reach, made failure seem both a reasonable and sublime occupation: ambition, particularly, is a sin against the abiding rush of a river. But I'll confess, I wasn't even in the water when I thought this; I was still standing in the high grass before barbed wire, preparing to crawl between its thorny knots, thinking this was no ordinary fence, but the door into the unknown world in all good stories, where spiritual journeys always start. Even the little scratch, the bit of blood on my arm, seemed a right and necessary beginning.

This feeling carried me straight through to the next day, north on the Bitterroot highway into Missoula, where in a slightly clearer but no less literary frame of mind I found a bona fide fly shop. Of course Missoula has at least a half dozen, all thriving, but this one had a proprietor who, through the big plate windows, bore a striking resemblance to a dear old friend of our family's, a man who in his lifetime had loved fishing and literature with equal passion. He'd point a finger straight up as if testing the wind, and quote somebody dead—in this case, Jean Cocteau: "The greatest beauty," he'd say, "is the beauty of failure." This made my parents nervous: it was un-American to embrace failure. But he gave me my first great books, among them *Moby Dick* and Turgenev's *Sketches from a Hunter's Notebook.* Not until years after his death would I discover that he'd wanted to write, that all his quotes contained a secret bitter message aimed at himself.

I looked at this owner innocently eating his corned beef sandwich and saw destiny in the coincidence of his familiar bald spot, his heavy glasses, his capable, square-fingered hands. Magically, no one else was in the shop for the moment, and when he saw me, he beckoned me in and spoke in a voice as miraculously gruff and East Coast as my old mentor, and took me around to all the cases, shaking his head grimly at my plain old monofilament and box of tattered wet flies while I privately misted over with nostalgia. In real life, I was apparently staring at some little hooks tied with red and gold thread, and he waved his hand disparagingly. "Sure," he said. "That's the San Juan worm, and it works just fine, but as a beginner, what you really want is a dry fly, so you can see the trout come up for it. That's what'll knock you out."

So I bought from him a half-dozen dries, a tapered leader, and some 6X tippet, all the time feeling a kind of warmth spreading in me, a great access of trust, of *home.* He threw in an extra Parachute Adams and a map of Rock Creek with his own favorite spots circled here and there. "Don't fool around up there," he said sternly. "Just stop at the first access point you find." Now, I thought, *now* I'm on track. But as I left the counter, I saw him turn with great comic enthusiasm to two young men who had just entered the shop. To him I was no hero at all, just one more dazed novice with shaking hands and weak terminology. God only knew what he was telling them now.

Back in the car, I fought the urge to go home, to give up the quest for now. But in my hand I held the map of the next mystery: a world-class fishery I'd never seen. I had the right leader, the right flies, and only 26 miles to go. I followed my guide's directions unswervingly. I stopped at the first access point and read the water; I even got my leader a tiny way out. No hits, but it was enough just to know I had tapered leader now, and after a few hours, I was sweetly exhausted by my little progress. The day passed beautifully, uneventfully, in that narrow canyon of building clouds and slate-colored water, a cool wind coming down the valley as the summer took its own first, minute turn toward fall. I'd been there to see it go, and this felt like enough adventure for one day.

It was then, in the cool of late afternoon, in a dark little glade into which leaves dropped with a mysterious living patter, that I sat down on my tailgate and set my keys beside me where I could not possibly forget them. I had begun to eat my Wheat Thins when I heard a thrashing in the woods behind me. Into view came a short heavy-set man with a red beard, an invader lumbering toward me with spinning rod and cooler. Behind him trailed an ancient, bent woman in giant rubber boots, a long wool skirt, and a kerchief around her head— a dream-babushka straight out of Turgenev's *Sketches*. She had the look of the old crone in fairy tales, the one who delivers the crucial if cryptic message, or opens the right gate, hitherto unnoticed. But no. The babushka retreated into the forest, and the man lumbered closer. I was pulling off my hip-boots when he began to speak in a garbled voice, with an accent deeper than deep South. He wanted to know how I'd done, what I was using. Parachute Adams, I said. He smirked and sprang the latch on his cooler, where a twenty-inch Brown trout lay cramped and faded against the dirty white. He addressed me again in that ferocious accent.

"Juh bring yer bait?" he asked.

"Illegal here," I said coolly.

"It's just un expression," he replied, rolling his eyes a little. "I mean yer bait box with yer minner muddlers and yer big woolly buggers. They're only eatin' the big stuff now, and they're hidin in the troughs. Din't juh notice the eagles?"

I looked politely into the sky, took another Wheat Thin. He rocked on his heels and snapped the cooler shut with a little violence. He was, I suspect, a man who did not like mysteries, particularly.

"Yer fixin ta leave yer keys," he said, pointing down at my bumper.

I tried to make the best of it, tried to convert this dirty moment as quickly as possible into story. This would be the nadir, this the dragon and the darkest moment of the heroic cycle. But I couldn't; I was depressed as hell. Something about the fading light, the dead fish in the cooler, the reminder, smack in the middle of a lyrical analysis, of the ugly side of failure: the trout lying trapped and flatly dead between his condescending teachings and my stubborn ignorance. It was too dark to go back out into the river again, and he stood there, quite clearly waiting to see me leave, as if he'd been sent to take up the last available light. The river was aloof now, cool and secretive, no risers, not a ripple in the troughs, the eagles gone up to their roosts.

"Well, I better get goin'," he said. "Don't forget them keys."

I waited there until I could no longer hear his boots crushing the brittle leaves, until I could no longer see his white cooler, that awful beacon, floating backward through the darkening woods. When it was quiet, I got back in the car and headed out Rock Creek Road, back toward Missoula. But I couldn't believe the story was over, so bleakly, hopelessly, finished. I was starved for a better ending. And lo, as if in answer, there rose up before me the Rock Creek Fly Shop, which, in my haste to get streamside, I'd missed on the way in. At the very least, I told myself, just use the bathroom, grab a soda, ask what these guys would have used.

I stumbled in, Eve expelled from the river for not knowing that the trout were lying in the troughs because of eagles, and eatin' only minner muddlers. I nodded at the man behind the counter, and tried to look like I knew my way around, but I couldn't see a rest room door anywhere.

"Lady," he said. "If it had teeth it would jump up and bite you."

"Just tell me where it is, right now," I said tensely.

He pointed behind me.

When I came out of the rest room he smiled. "You look tired," he said. "What were you using—I hear they're pulling in the big browns like nobody's business!" I shook my head and he slapped his hands on the counter. "You were using *what?*" he said. "What joker told you to use a dry on a day like this?" He paused dramatically, hand on the phone, ready to dial 911. "It's only big stuff now, they're only eatin' big stuff." Again, the sad shake of the head, the unspoken message that if you'd only asked him first instead of The Guys in Town, you'd be rich with fish, hell, Missoula's 26 miles away, what do they know?

It occurred to me that I should stop taking advice for a while, that all advice was suspect, hopelessly rooted in some deep and complicated tangle of pride and secret regret that rose up to meet the susceptible customer with her own deep and complicated tangle of pride and secret regret.

But the proprietor had stopped talking, and was looking at me as if I'd asked him a deep theological question. "Wait a minute," he said. "Come with me." He beckoned me away from the Jerky and the Wheat Thins and the cases of flies, around a corner to another room entirely—one I would never have guessed was there. In this room a potbellied woodstove hissed and crackled. A family was seated around the stove: two brothers in red flannel shirts and jeans were cleaning their guns; a young woman, with cheeks flushed from the heat of the stove, was knitting; a baby, also red-faced, with its knitted cap fallen low over one eye, lay regal and stunned in its swaddling.

The proprietor seated himself at a round table piled high with yarn, feathers, fur and thread. "Here we go," he said. He wound red chenille around the shank of a hook, and burned both ends with a match. "I call it the Poor Man's San Juan Worm," he said. "It has no class, but when all else fails—"

I didn't leave right away. I held myself still, welcomed, if not into the life of the river, then a step closer to it. It was like falling into a fine old painting of peasant life, where there's a golden light coming from some window you can't see. The dog sleeps, the hunters pause over their guns, the baby lies amazed under the golden light. We are at the beginning again, with Rock Creek just outside, moving swiftly through its canyon as the dark comes on in earnest. Cocteau would approve, and so would my old mentor: by failing to catch trout, look at the gift you've been granted.

Never mind that on my next visit to Missoula, the owner of the fly shop will look at my San Juan Worm and say accusingly, "Where the hell did you get this? It's all wrong. Who made it?" My host at Rock Creek must have known this would happen, because as he handed me the finished fly, he smiled the brief, cramped smile of the failed artist, the wise teacher.

54

"Just a little present," he said. "Since you tried so hard. Just promise me you won't tell the guys in Missoula who made it. They'd have my head."

Trout

John Gierach

Let's say you're nymph-fishing on Colorado's South Platte River. You've hiked up into the canyon where those deliciously deep potholes are—the big-fish water—but have found that today the trout are working the shallow, fast runs. It took you two hours to figure that out, but it's a good sign. They're hungry and, as your partner says, they are "looking up." You're fishing a scud pattern, not *the* scud pattern, but one you worked out yourself. The differences are minute but are enough to make it your fly and you are catching fish on it, which is highly satisfactory.

You're working the near edge of a fast rip about thirty yards above a strong plunge pool, flipping the weighted nymph rig upstream and following its descent with the rod tip. Your concentration is imperfect as you toy with the idea that this is okay, a fascinating and demanding way to fish, actually, but that too many days of it in a row could make you homesick for the easy grace of real fly casting.

At the little jiggle in the leader that was just a hair too intelligent looking to be nothing but current or a rock, you raise the rod to set the hook, and there's weight. And then there's movement—it's a fish.

It's a big fish, not wiggling, but boring, shaking its head in puzzlement and aggravation, but not in fear. It's impressive.

Almost lazily, the trout rises from the bottom into the faster current near the surface, rolls into the rip, and is off downstream. What you feel is more weight than fight, and the wings of panic begin to flutter around your throat. This is the once- or twice-a-year "oh-shit" fish. You should have tried to catch a glimpse of him when he turned—the only glimpse you may get—but it all happened so fast. No it didn't. It actually happened rather slowly, almost lazily, as you just pointed out.

You are careful (too careful? not careful enough?). The hook is a stout, heavy-wire number 10, but the tippet is only a 5x, about 4-pound test. The rod is an 8½-foot cane with plenty of backbone in the butt, but with a nicely sensitive tip (catalog talk, but true). The drag on the reel is set light, and line is leaving it smoothly. You drop the rod to half-mast to give the fish his head and are, in fact, doing everything right. It's hopeless.

The trout is far downstream now, on the far side of the rip and the plunge, but the local topography makes it impossible for you to follow. The line is bellied, no longer pointing at the fish.

At some point you are struck by the knowledge that the trout—that enormous trout—is no longer attached to you and all your expensive tackle, though you missed the exact moment of separation. You reel in to find that he did not throw the hook but broke you off fairly against the weight of the river. You get a mental snapshot of your fly hanging in the hooked jaw of a heavy . . . what? A rainbow? More likely a brown. You'll never know.

Losing a fish like that is hard. Sure, you were going to release him anyway, but that's not the point. The plan was to be magnanimous in victory. You ask yourself, was it my fault? A typically analytical question. You can avoid it with poetry of the "it's just nice to be out fishing" variety, or you can soften it with the many levels of technical evasion, but there's finally only one answer: of course it was your fault, who else's fault would it be?

Your partner is out of sight and, although you would have hollered and screamed for him and his camera had you landed the fish, it's not even worth going to find him, now. When you finally meet in the course of leapfrogging down the canyon, you'll say that a while ago you executed an L.D.R. (long distance release) on a hawg, which will summarize the event as well as anything else you could say.

A trout, on this continent at least, is a rainbow, golden, brookie, brown, cutthroat, or some subspecies or hybrid of the above, though every fly fisher is secretly delighted that the brook trout isn't a trout at all, but rather a kind of char, not that it matters. ·

Much is actually known about trout and much more is suspected. The serious fly fisherman's knowledge of these fish draws heavily on science, especially the easygoing, slightly bemused, English-style naturalism of the last century, but it periodically leaves the bare facts behind to take long voyages into anthropomorphism and sheer poetry. Trout are said to be angry, curious, shy, belligerent, or whatever; or it's suggested that when one takes your Adams with a different rise form than he's using on the Blue-winged Olives he "thought" it was a caddisfly. Cold science tells us that a trout's pea-sized brain is not capable of anything like reason or emotion. That's probably true enough, but in the defense of creative thinking, I have a comment and a question: actions speak louder than words and, if they're so dumb, how come they can be so hard to catch?

The myth of the smart trout was invented by fishermen as a kind of implied self-aggrandizement. To be unable to hook the wise old brown trout is one thing, but to be outsmarted by some slimy, cold-blooded, subreptilian creature with only the dullest glimmerings of awareness is, if not degrading, then at least something you don't want spread around. Trout are smart, boy, real smart.

The way we perceive trout is probably as faulty, from a factual standpoint, as the way they see us, but our folksy ideas about them are useful and are, in that sense, correct. If you tie a streamer fly and fish it in a way designed to make spawning brown trout "mad" and, in the course of events, manage to hook a few fish, then those fish were, by God, mad. End of discussion.

Let's say a fisheries biologist tells you that his studies, and the studies of others, demonstrate that brook trout are not piscivorous; that is, they don't eat other fish. To that you counter that you have caught countless brook trout on streamers (fish imitations), that many of the now-standard American streamer patterns were developed around the wild brook trout fisheries of the East, and that, further, fly fishermen have believed brook trout to be fish-eaters for nigh these many generations.

"Well," he says, "we all know brookies are stupid."

Thank you, Mister Science.

Finally, the things fishermen know about trout aren't facts but articles of faith. Brook trout may or may not eat fish, but they bite streamers. You can't even use the scientific method because the results of field testing are always suspect. There are too many variables and the next guy to come along may well prove an opposing theory beyond the shadow of a doubt.

The hatch is the Blue-winged Olive so common in the West. It's a perfect emergence from the fly fisher's point of view: heavy enough to move all but the very largest of the trout but not so heavy that your pitiful imitation is lost in such a crowd of bugs that the surface of the stream seems fuzzy. Oh yes, hatches can be too good.

When the rise began you fished a #18 dark nymph pattern squeezed wet so it would drift just a fraction of an inch below the surface. This copies the emerging nymph at that point where it has reached the surface but has not yet hatched into the winged fly. Early on in the hatch, these are the bugs that are the most readily available to the fish, the ones they're probably taking even though at first glance it looks like they're rising to dry flies. The difference in position between an emerging nymph and a floating fly is the almost nonexistent thickness of the surface film of the water, and there is often zero difference between the trout's rise forms.

When the hatch progresses to the point where there are more winged flies on the water than emerging nymphs, you switch to the dry fly, only a few minutes after most of the trout have. There are two mayflies on the water now, identical except that one is about a size 18 and the other, the more numerous, is more like a #22. The larger is the *Baetis* and the smaller is the *Pseudocloeon.* You heard that from the local expert and looked up the spellings in *Hatches,* by Caucci and Nastasi. It sounds good, but what it means is that you fish either the Blue-winged Olive or the Adams in a size 20, to split the difference.

The fish are an almost uniform 14 to 16 inches—rainbows with a strong silvery cast to them, bodies fatter than most stream fish, with tiny little heads. They are wild and healthy, and you would drive five times farther than you did to fish here.

They're rising everywhere now. In the slower water they're dancing and darting, suspending for a few seconds now and then as if to catch their breath. They will move several inches for your fly, taking it matter-of-factly, completely fooled, but leaving you only a single, precise instant that won't be too early or too late to strike. This has you wound up like the E string on a pawnshop guitar.

In the faster water they are all but invisible, but they're out there because there are enough bugs to make them buck the current. They come up from the bottom through two feet of water, taking the fly with such grace and lack of hesitation that the little blip on the surface seems unconnected with that fluid arc of greenish, pinkish, silvery light in the riffle.

You are on, hot, wired. You've caught so many trout that the occasional missed strike is a little joke between you and the fish. This is the exception rather than the rule—the time when everything comes together—but it feels comfortable, like it happens all the time. A hint of greed creeps in. You would like, maybe, a little bigger trout, and to that end you work the far bank. Still, though the trout are now almost part of a process rather than individual victories, you admire each one momentarily before releasing it and going confidently for another.

It's late in the hatch now. Most of the river is in shadow, and the remaining light has a golden, autumnal cast to it. The little rusty-brownish spinners could come on now. This could last. But it's too perfect; it *can't* last.

Trout are wonderfully hydrodynamic creatures who can dart and hover in currents in which we humans have trouble just keeping our footing. They are torpedo shaped, designed for moving water, and behave like eyewitnesses say U.F.O.s do, with sudden stops from high speeds, ninety-degree turns, such sudden accelerations that they seem to just vanish. They seem delicate at times but will turn around and flourish in conditions that look impossibly harsh. They like things clean and cold.

They are brilliantly, often outrageously, colored (the wild ones, anyway) and are a pure and simple joy to behold, though they can be damned hard to see in the water. Even the most gorgeously colored fish are as dark and mottled on the back as the finest U.S. Army–issue jungle camouflage to hide them from predators from above: herons, kingfishers, ospreys, and—only recently in evolutionary terms—you and me. Then there are those rare times when the light and everything else is just right, when they're as exposed as birds in the sky, in open water under bright sun as if they were in paradise. At such times they can look black. You feel like a voyeur, delighted with a view of something you have no right to see; but don't feel too guilty—they'll spook at your first cast.

In one sense trout are perfectly adapted working parts of a stream, a way of turning water, sunlight, oxygen, and protein into consciousness. They feed on the aquatic insects when those bugs are active, and they all but shut down metabolically when they're not. They find glitches in the current where, even in the wildest water, they can lounge indefinitely by now and then lazily paddling a pectoral fin. They have the flawless competence that even the lower mammals have

lost by getting to be too smart. They operate at
the edges of things: fast and slow currents, deep
and shallow water, air and stream, light and darkness, and the angler who understands that is well on his way to
knowing what he's doing.

In another sense, trout are so incongruously pretty as to seem otherworldly:
that metallic brightness, the pinks and oranges and yellows—and the spots. One
of the finest things about catching a trout is being able to turn it sideways and just
look at it. How can so much color and vibrancy be generated by clear water, gray
rocks, and brown bugs? Trout are among those creatures who are one hell of a lot
prettier than they need to be. They can get you to wondering about the hidden
workings of reality.

Releasing trout is a difficult idea to get hold of at first. It doesn't seem to make
sense. You want the meat; you want the *proof.*

In the beginning, catching a trout on a fly is one of those things you have to
do before you actually come to believe it's possible. Those first maddening weeks
or months with a fly rod make other fly casters seem like the guy in the circus
who can put the soles of his feet flat on the top of his head. Sure, *he* can do it. If
you don't flip out and go back to the spinning rod, you eventually find that it can
be done, though the gap between the first time you take trout on a fly rod and the
second time can be so wide you come to wonder if it ever really happened. It's easy
to lose the clarity of that initial vision. You hear it all the time: "I tried fly fishing;
couldn't get the hang of it."

You keep the early trout (anyone who doesn't is too saintly to be normal) but
in time you begin to see the virtue of releasing the wild fish. The logic is infalli-
ble: if you kill him, he's gone; if you release him he's still there. You can think of
it in terms of recycling, low impact, all the properly futuristic phrases.

With some practice it's easy to do correctly. Smaller trout can be landed
quickly—the barbless hook is turned out with a practiced motion of the wrist, and
it darts away, baffled but unharmed. You haven't lifted him from the water or even
touched him.

Larger fish require more handling. You're careful not to lift them by the gill covers or squeeze them too much, causing internal damage. A landing net with a soft
cotton-mesh bag helps. Big fish played to exhaustion on tackle that's unavoidably
too light are carefully resuscitated (held gently in the current and pumped until

they get their wind back and can swim off under their own steam). They seem dazed, and you know that if they were stressed too much, with too much lactic acid built up in their systems, they'll eventually die. It's something to wonder about. Some of your released fish have probably expired later, but you don't know enough about it to determine the actual medical condition of any particular one.

It begins to feel good, the heft and muscle tension of a bright, pretty, live trout held lightly in the cold water. It's like a mild electric shock without the pain. Finally, there's not even an instant of remorse when they dart away. At some point our former values change ends; the bigger the trout, the more satisfying the release. Having all but lost your taste for fish, you begin to release everything— wild fish, stockers, stunted brook trout, whitefish, bluegills—with an air of right-eousness that pains many of those around you.

At some point you become an absolute snot about it. You are incensed that even staunch antihunters aren't bothered by the killing of fish, that vegetarians will bend the rules for seafood. This, you come to realize, is because trout are not seen as cute by the general population, though of course they are wrong. You begin to feel misunderstood.

That feeling can go on for years, and in some anglers it calcifies into the belief that killing a trout is murder. But maybe one day, without giving it much thought, you go down to the reservoir, after having spotted the hatchery truck there in the morning, and bag a limit of stockers (pale, sickly looking things with faint purplish stripes where the pink stripe would be on a wild rainbow). It doesn't feel half bad.

Breaded with yellow cornmeal and flour and fried in butter, they're okay, not unlike fishsticks, but with a livery undertaste.

That same season, or perhaps the next, you take a brace of wild fish for what you refer to as a "ceremonial" camp dinner, carefully pointing out that they are small brook trout from overpopulated water. They taste good. They taste wonderful.

You come to realize that you have to kill some now and then because this whole business of studying, stalking, outsmarting, and overpowering game is *about* death and killing. Take two (three, if they're small) coldly and efficiently, and if you comment on it at all, say something like, "That there is a nice mess of fish."

You still release most of the trout you catch, even in waters where that's not the law, but it's no longer a public gesture. Now it's just what pleases you. When they're big and pretty, you take a photograph, with Kodachrome for the hot colors.

The river was the Henry's Fork in Southern Idaho, at a place that I have been politely asked not to describe. I'll try not to. It's not far upstream from the spot where Archie (A.K.) Best and I saw a yard-long rainbow try to eat a blackbird who was standing at the end of a sweeper picking off Brown Drakes. Honest. Biggest trout either of us had ever seen. The bird got away.

This was the following year and, hunting for the Brown Drake hatch that never materialized, we located another big trout, maybe 25 inches long (maybe longer, it's hard to tell), who was unbelievably feeding on #18 Pale Morning Dun spinners. Only on a bug factory like the Henry's Fork would a fish of that size still be interested in little mayflies. We decided it would be great fun to hook a trout like that on a dry fly and, say, a 5x tippet. I say "hook." We never discussed how we'd land it and I doubt either of us seriously considered it could be done. Still, with all that open water, slow current, and plenty of backing . . . It would have been something.

It was early June. The Pale Morning Duns were coming off, with simultaneous spinner falls and a smattering of Green Drakes that the fish would switch to when they showed up. Some locals and some hot-dog tourists said the fishing was "slow." A. K. and I wondered what the hell they wanted.

By day we fished in the crowd, sometimes taking an afternoon break to hit the campground, ease out, sip coffee, tie some flies. One day we went up to another stream and caught some little rainbows and brookies for lunch. As we do on the Henry's Fork, we discussed the possibility of taking a day and hitting the Madison or the Teton, or even the Warm River, but never went. We were Henry's Fork junkies on a typical extended trip.

By night (early evening, actually) we would drive to a certain turnoff and then walk to a certain spot where the impossibly big rainbow would be rising to the spinner fall like clockwork. We had Rusty Spinners, Cream Spinners, quill-bodied and dubbed-bodied spinners, spinners with poly wings and hackle-tip wings and clipped-hackle wings, and, for later, Michigan Chocolate spinners for that sharp, dark silhouette against the night sky.

We were fishing rods we'd each built up from identical blanks, old 9-foot, 6-weight waterseals. They were heavy rods, but slow and powerful, just what one would need to land that heavy a trout on a little fly and light tippet. We'd thought this out very well.

For five, maybe six, nights we showed up regularly at that spot and returned to the campground just as the last few friendship fires were down to coals. It would be too late to start anything, so we'd sit on the ground around our cold fire pit, sipping a beer before turning in and muttering arcanely about the fish, the flies, the insects, leader diameters, knots, and the hoped-for commencement of the Brown Drake hatch that we thought might give us a real crack at *The Trout*. If he (she, probably, but I can't help thinking of big trout as masculine) was taking the little spinners, he'd surely move for the huge #10 Drakes. The big flies would help, and their nighttime emergence and large size would let us go to heavier leaders. In our quiet madness we actually tried to quantify how much of an advantage that would give us. It was time. It could happen any night now. Exactly one year ago the hatch had been on.

Our colleagues at the campground figured we had something going—probably fishwise, possibly womanwise—but, although they sometimes hedged around it a little, they never actually came out and asked. Night-fishers are seen as a distinctly antisocial breed and are best not pushed.

We would take turns casting to *The Trout*, alternating who started first on successive nights. We were perfect gentlemen about it, wishing each other well with complete unselfishness, and then cringing with covetous greed as the other guy worked the fish. One night I broke down and fished a big, weighted Brown Drake nymph and then, later, an enormous streamer on an Ox leader. Not even a bump. A.K. stayed righteous with the dry fly.

Another night a mackenzie boat with a guide and two sports came down from upriver. The guide obviously knew about the fish and wanted to put his clients over it, either because he thought they were good enough to do some business or just to blow their minds. He was pulling for the channel when he spotted me casting from a kneeling crouch and A.K. sitting cross-legged next to me waiting for me to relinquish my turn.

The guide gave us only the briefest sour look and then delivered the obligatory we're-all-in-this-together-good-luck wave.

Two turkeys on the big trout. Damn!

During the course of those evenings we each hooked that fish once and were each summarily, almost casually, broken off, causing our estimation of his size to be revised upwards to the point where inches and pounds became meaningless— a fish of which dreams are made, known to the local guides.

You could hear him rising through the layered silence of the stream: "GLUP." He'd start rising late, when the spinner fall was down nicely and the smaller fish were already working.

63

The smaller fish. We caught a few of those, measuring up to 19 and 22 inches, our two largest. Such is the capacity of the human mind to compare one thing to another, thus missing the moment and thinking of a 22-inch trout as a little fish.

Exactly what a trout is, not to mention its considerable significance, is difficult to convey to someone who doesn't fish for them with a fly rod. There's the biology and taxonomy, photographs, paintings, and the long history of the sport, but what the nonangler is incapable of grasping is that, although individual fish clearly exist, *The Trout* remains a legendary creature. I'm talking about those incredible fish that we see but can't catch, or don't even see but still believe in. The *big* trout—another concept the nonfisherman thinks he understands but doesn't.

What constitutes a big trout is a relative thing, regardless of the efforts of some to make it otherwise. You'll now and then hear a fly fisher say a trout isn't really big until it's 20 inches long, a statement I invariably take to be jet-set bullshit, although I'll grant you that 20 inches is a nice, round figure. Fisheries managers often refuse to consider a piece of water as gold medal (or blue ribbon, or whatever) unless it demonstrably contains x percentage of trout over x inches in length. The magazines are filled with photos of huge, dripping trout, the ones you'll catch if you'll only master the following technique.

In another camp are the fishermen who claim not to care how big a trout is. "It's the challenge," they'll say, "the flies, the casting, the manner and method. Nothing wrong with a foot-long trout. Oh, and the scenery, and the birds singing, etc." I use that line myself and, like most of us, I sincerely believe it, act upon it regularly, and am happy, but tell me you know where the hawgs are and I'll follow you through hell.

Fly fishing for trout is a sport that depends not so much on catching the fish as on their mere presence and on the fact that you do, now and again, catch some. As for their size, the bigger they are, the better, to be honest about it, though all that stuff about the manner and the method and the birds singing isn't entirely compensatory.

The Best Thing About Trout

A Morality Play in Four Acts About Fish Who Are,
Sometimes, Almost as Selective as Fishermen

Datus C. Proper

THERE IS AN ANGLER ON STAGE as the curtain rises on a wooded bend of the Potomac River (which is a peculiar place to begin a drama about selective trout). The sky is orange haze, too thick for breathing and too thin for swimming. Sand scrunches around in the angler's basketball shoes; water a little cooler than blood circulates through his trousers; a stringer with some yellowbelly sunfish on it tugs from his belt. They have been kept because they taste better than smallmouth bass. The bass have been hitting too, but they usually take the little metal lure at the end of the line, while the sunfish prefer a wet fly tied above the lure as a dropper. The whole outfit is a hybrid. The line is 4-pound monofilament cast from a little Alcedo spinning reel that is taped to the grip of an old fiberglass fly rod.

As the sun sets and the haze darkens, a few big, pale mayfly duns start coming down the water. The rings of rising fish appear. The lure works better than ever now, because the bass hit it right under the surface instead of waiting for it to jig along the bottom. But the angler thinks he's missing something even if the fish

don't. As the rings grow more abundant, he switches to a fly line and starts covering the rises. A big Light Cahill dry fly appeals to the fish but drowns quickly.
A cork popper works too. Then, just before leaving, the angler puts on a streamer and fishes it across and downstream, having read somewhere that the big fish
lie deeper, waiting to catch the little risers. Maybe. The bass hit the streamer as
well as the dry fly, but the biggest fish of the evening is not big enough to eat the
smallest rising sunfish.

The truth seems to be that these fish don't care a lot what fly—or lure—is
used, as long as they are in a mood to feed and the victim will fit into their mouths.
Even though natural insects start the rise, a little piece of chromed metal works as
well as something with a Latin name. But fly fishing is more fun. At least, it's
almost fly fishing. There's the natural fly, the ring of the rise, the thick line in the
air, the float with an artificial fly, another rise, the strike, and the fish tugging
against a long rod. All of the ingredients of fly fishing.

Except one. But that one missing ingredient is enough, in the end, to persuade
the angler to get up at four in the morning and drive to a trout stream that's three
times as far away.

Act II is set about sixty degrees farther south and six thousand feet higher, near
the Brazilian resort town of Campos do Jordão. The air smells better here. The
angler pulls off a dirt track and parks, then hikes downhill, which is where the
trout streams hide out in any part of the world. His pants get wet from dew and
greasy from the billy-goat-beard grass. As he hikes downward, the grass yields to
Araucaria pine, and then to mossy jungle. The easiest way to penetrate that is to
wade up a brook called Canhambora.

This time there is no fly reel anywhere in the angler's vest. He has never seen
a surface-feeding fish here and it's hard to cast up through the clutching bamboo,
even with a five-foot spinning rod. Before lunch he hooks one trout, loses it in a
snag, and is about ready to quit for the day when he sees the unexpected: a rise.
Then another, about thirty feet upstream. Drab little duns are trickling down the
stream and a rainbow is taking them. Now here is a coincidence: the only fly fisherman in all of Brazil is present in the only place where a trout is taking
mayflies—and the fisherman has no fly tackle.

Eventually, he casts his smallest lure twenty feet above the rising trout and
retrieves, $1/16$-ounce spinner high in the water, flickering right in the path the
duns have pointed out. The trout quivers and sinks a little lower, clearly fright-

ened. It is two minutes before the fish takes a dun again and, on the next pass of the lure, the rainbow flees.

Why? The angler is reasonably sure that the little lure would have been taken if only the fish had not been looking for another mayfly. But the trout's opinion was definitive, as it usually is, and the score for the day remains: fish two, fisherman zero. On the long hike back uphill, the angler does not like the score, but he likes the trout. What other fish would introduce an American to the Canhambora? And then, in the bargain, give him a lesson in the fitness of things?

Trout have a lot of virtues, but on most of them they have no monopoly. Take beauty, for example: Woodcock are as pretty as trout and much warmer, and you find woodcock where the leaves are turning color. A woodcock covert does as much for the senses as a trout stream.

Trout are not even the only fish that are, sometimes, selective about their food. Grayling and Rocky Mountain whitefish behave that way, but not as often, and maybe you have found bass being selective (though I don't think I have). For all I know, the upland streams of Tahiti may have a fish that behaves like a brown trout, but no one has written much about it. People have written uncounted millions of words on trout fishing, and the trout's peculiar feeding habits account for much of the literature. We cannot identify the Macedonian stream that Aelian wrote about in the third century or what kind of natural fly he may have been describing, but he was clearly reporting on fishing with an imitative fly. When the *Treatyse of Fishing With An Angle* appeared in English in the fifteenth century, one of its premises was that artificial flies should resemble the trout's natural food. The same assumption underlies the early Spanish literature, which seems unrelated to the English.

67

So, if you will accept literary evidence, the best thing about trout is the oddly discerning way in which they may choose to feed. This trait is doubly puzzling because trout do not appear to have been designed for the task. A biologist might not agree with this, but if I were seeing a two-pound brown trout for the first time, I would not guess that he had reached his size by eating tiny insects. Trout, like black bass, have big mouths, and nature does not usually provide physical equipment without a reason. I would surmise that a fish shaped like the trout would specialize in minnows or frogs or mice. And of course trout do eat such creatures, but it's remarkable how often they prefer small insects instead. I like to take pictures of trout with little artificial flies showing as dots on big jaws: It looks like such a miraculous feat.

Miracle or not, I am grateful for the trout's diet, because insects are needed, lots of them, to make a fish most selective. In order to fill his stomach with mayflies, a trout may have to feed hundreds of times, and he gets clever at it.

It is because of this unusual manner of feeding that the pursuit of trout has been called an "intellectual passion." No one has called 'coon hunting or perch fishing intellectual passions, and I wouldn't venture to make a case for woodcock. They arouse fierce but identical passions in me and my dog, and at least one of us is no intellectual.

The peculiar feeding habits of trout cause those of us who pursue them to carry around hooks dressed very differently from those of non-trout anglers. We often call these creations "flies" even when—as in the case of streamers—we are trying to imitate little fish instead of insects. (We would, it seems, rather stretch the language than risk confusion with pike fishermen.) Mind you, it is impossible to find a trout that shares all the tastes of trout-fishers, and it is not even as easy as you might suppose to find one that is highly selective. If "selective" is to mean anything, it has to mean more than "hard to catch." Bass and muskellunge are hard to catch, too, but for different reasons.

68

Perhaps I've missed something, but I don't recall that any angler, in the centuries of writing, has said just what selectivity does mean. We'll try here, later on. First let's look at some of the assumptions on which fishes and fishers agree—or disagree.

There is, for example, a friend of mine who has been known to float Quill Gordons over a kind of degenerate, peroxide-blonde rainbow that they breed in West Virginia. The fly has to be a Quill Gordon because that is what might be hatching in April, and by May the predators will have cleaned out any fish that were bred to be conspicuous. The Quill Gordon says a lot about the angler but not much about the trout, who are not even bright enough to be selective to hatchery pellets.

And how about the Brazilian trout in Act II? He might have taken any floating fly of about the right size, if the angler had given him a chance. If he had accepted, say, a Royal Coachman instead of a Quill Gordon, how many anglers would call that selectivity? Never mind, for now. At least the Brazilian rainbow knew the difference between mayfly and metal trinket. Thanks to fish like him, there is a sport aspiring to Quill Gordons instead of Cheez-Eggs. Granted that trout anglers do not invariably need hexagonal bamboo rods, hundreds of flies, boxes with little flippy lids to hold the flies, and vests with twenty-two pockets each to store the boxes. The equipment at least satisfies functional needs as well as our emotions.

The trout takes us seriously, you and me, but the human audience can be counted on to giggle as we waddle upstream in full felt-soled armor, searching for something small, shy, and primitive. We are a parody waiting to happen. The critics know more about theater than trout, and they write us up as Falstaffs in bulging vests. But there is not much trout-fishing satire that is good enough to sting. A clever satirist has to understand motivations, and I can't name one who has perceived that we see ourselves as supporting actors in a morality play. The paraphernalia and the sweat in our waders are offerings—spurned, perhaps, but extended in fervor. We are trying, with our clumsy fingers in the fly-box, to be guided by nature instead of superstition. We have been trying for centuries. And it is all because of selectivity.

Thanks, trout.

For Act III the backdrop changes to lodgepole pines, grass curing to the hue of autumn sun, and the long riffle that is the Madison River. The angler feels as small as he looks, with only a raven's echo for company, but he hopes for a big trout. There aren't many. The fall run from Hebgen Lake is mostly made up of fish closer to one pound than two: splendid on light tackle in the summer, but short work for a steelhead rod. The heavy gear is, however, useful for pitching the big, weighted object at the end of the leader, which is intended to represent a stonefly nymph.

Under another sky this might be drudgery, because there are long stretches with ponderous casting and no fish. When located, the trout—browns and a few fall-run rainbows—take innocently. They haven't seen many flies with hooks in them. Then, in the first moments of each fight, the trout hangs deep against the current, the rod develops a pregnant belly and the angler has a minute to feel the heartbeat and hope that this is the one he wanted. In the end, there is a trout who jerks more slowly than the others and lasts longer coming to the net. This is not the summer's most difficult fish but it is the biggest—four pounds plus, and perfect. There is no trace of spawning color yet to dull sides shining like the sun-gold grass. If Hebgen Lake were salt water, this fish would carry sea lice.

There are lots of natural stonefly nymphs in the Madison, so you might consider these trout selective. You might except that three-quarters of them take a little wet fly sticking out from a dropper higher up the leader. When the angler changes the stonefly nymph on the point to a weighted streamer, the trout don't care much for that, either. Next the angler spoons some stomachs to see whether any food in them resembles the little wet fly—and finds no food at all. These lake-run fish, like salmon, are responding to something besides a need for nutrition.

Of course, the fish might take the big point fly more often if there were no easily available alternative on the dropper. Fall-run Madison trout often do take streamers and nymphs that look like stoneflies. But in this Act the big creations at the end of the leader serve mainly as sinkers, giving the dropper some kind of behavior the trout like. Most fishermen who use droppers have had similar experiences.

The little dropper, then, has two functions. First, it catches fish; and second, it keeps the fisherman honest about selectivity.

The moral of Act III is that selectivity is something you cannot presume, if you want to play square in your game with nature. Suppose that the angler had fished with the stonefly nymph alone—no dropper. Suppose he had not checked stomach contents. Suppose he had caught fish anyhow (which is probable) and suppose, finally, that he had gone home and talked about how those fish loved stoneflies. He would have been wrong. The little dropper gave the trout a chance to reject the stonefly hypothesis, and most of them did.

Selectivity must be proved, or (more frequently) disproved, not by what fish eat but by what they reject. The point about rejection is central, so let's look at what the dictionary says. To select (according to the American Heritage dictionary) means "to choose from among several, pick out." And selective means "of or characterized by selection; discriminating." Now, clearly, when one item from among several is picked out, there must be other items that are not picked out, or rejected. A trout who eats everything readily available is not making a selection.

Does the point seem obvious? Not to one fisherman—a good one—who wrote this dissenting opinion: "Selectivity is, in fact, a built-in response to the great abundance of any one food organism, subaquatic or floating on the film." Now this is a simple, comfortable approach. Unfortunately, it does not work, either in the dictionary or on the stream. If you read the quoted sentence again, you will see that it makes no reference to choice, or selection. And, in practical terms, a trout faced with "a great abundance of any one food organism" will very likely learn to eat it—thereby demonstrating opportunism, not selectivity. The fish may also be selective, but you cannot know that unless you give him repeated chances to choose between the insect on the water and some alternative food, real or fake, like your fly.

In practice, fish that have been taking a single kind of food may not be very selective. In the wilderness lakes of Yellowstone Park, for example, I seldom found trout (or grayling) that would refuse a fancy wet fly, even when they were feeding on scuds or midges. I think I know why the fish behaved as they did, but that's another story. We lack space here for many of the puzzles, such as why some trout are more selective than others and some conditions seem more likely to bring on a selective response.

On some waters, trout do regularly refuse well-fished flies, and that makes selectivity important to anglers. Fortunately, we can check on it, more easily than biologists. We may have to try a few flies to find out for sure what an individual trout rejects, but this we can do in a short time, before he switches from one food to another. Biologists must seine out a sample of everything drifting down a stream, which is a non-selective way to measure selectivity. Perhaps this is why biologists like to talk about the behavior of populations rather than individual fish. Choice, however, is an individual act, and trout are practical about it but by no means automatons. Suppose that one fish is taking spent spinners in midstream while another is waiting for ants to fall off a grassy bank. On the average, that population of two fish is non-selective, because it's taking half mayflies and half terrestrials. The angler—if he wants to catch much—may have to make a more precise call than that.

On the other hand, we anglers don't inspire as much confidence as biologists unless we're equally careful with our conclusions. Most of us do, I think, choose to be a little more strict than the dictionary with our usage. If, on some trip, the bass hit a Jitterbug three times more often than a Crazy Crawler, we don't usually claim that the bass are selective: we conclude only that the Jitterbug has some episodic appeal we don't understand. Similarly, I don't think that the Madison fish should be considered selective to a small dropper fly just because they took it three times out of four. Many other flies might have worked, if given a chance. The fish must have had their reasons for liking the dropper but we cannot understand them, because the trout were not taking any artificial food to which the natural could be related. Only an angler of very great faith would expect much selectivity from non-feeding fish.

In angling terms, I conceive of a selective fish as one that has been taking a single kind of food, expects to see another specimen of the same kind, will take it if it appears, but will be less likely to take any other kind of food. He then sees my artificial fly and decides that it is—or is not—what he has been expecting. (He will not, of course, take my fly if he realizes that it is an artificial, no matter how attractive.)

If you concur, let's try the following as an angler's definition:

Selectivity in fish is a preference for one kind of food as opposed to another that is readily available.

In Act IV, it takes the audience a while to stop coughing and realize that the theme of the background music is quietness. There is not even the rustle of the Madison, though another set of Montana ranges circles most of the backdrop. A spring creek filters noiselessly through watercress beds. The angler can hear the winnowing of a snipe hidden in the depths of a clear sky, and a sandhill crane groans about something two farms north. Once Paul Schullery (who has good ears) heard a trout swimming in this stream. Anybody can hear a fly line splatting down at the end of a cast, and wince. Probably the trout wince too, because they sidle upstream forty feet without looking at the angler's fly, and he realizes that this August morning isn't going to be easy. But at least the trout keep on rising. There are heavy ones in there, and they need a vast number of tiny mayflies and tinier midges to stay in condition.

This, finally, is the kind of limestone stream where you would expect the fish to be selective, as well as wary. And sometimes they oblige. The angler finds it helpful to match the mayflies in whatever stage the trout are taking—nymph, dun, spinner—and then to tie on a beetle when the rise is over, or perhaps a grasshopper if the wind comes up. When the Tricos are hatching, the fly has to be small. The occasional swirls after cranefly larvae call for something much larger and fast-moving. Always the fly has to come down behaving like the natural, at the right level.

Enter on stage Glenn Brackett. In a stream that many a good fisherman leave at the end of the day with a lemon-sucking smile, Glenn just slithers upstream catching fish. He doesn't talk much about his flies. They are well tied and small enough, but they mostly come in a multipurpose shape and any old color. I think his system is to pick up whichever one comes up first in the box: red in the body, last time I looked.

A successful subversive like Glenn can cause a fellow to question the whole philosophical underpinning of trout. Not that Glenn means to shake the faith— actually, he makes bamboo rods, looks like a trout fisherman, and tries not to show off his heretical flies. The stupid fish are the problem. How, when yellow duns are hatching, can trout ignore my respectable yellow imitation and take Glenn's red one? It goes to show you the dangers of asking what the fish think instead of what fishermen think. To hell with trout. They are primitive, cold-blooded, cannibalistic, low in I.Q. and, worst of all, grossly deficient in the good taste that characterizes anglers.

Still, there may be a magic that can save the old order.

Color. It is very strong magic, for fishermen, while trout seldom worry about it. And that, I think, is the kernel of the disagreement between trout and people.

I do not mean to say that trout always disregard color. They have excellent color vision—better than ours—and, personally, I think they use it sometimes to distinguish good food from bad. But the proposition is difficult to prove beyond question. The fact that trout have a certain ability does not mean that they invariably exercise it: we have already seen that they often specialize in insects, even though trout have evolved with a mouth that will accept larger food.

73

It seems to me that, in practice, the behavior of a fly usually matters more than color or any other feature to a trout. After behavior, size matters, and less frequently trout seem to insist on a plausible shape. So, in designing flies these days, I would argue that it makes less sense to be guided by color than by behavior, size, and shape. By this reasoning, Glenn Brackett's Act IV fly was not as subversive as it looked in the first red flush.

We fishermen, however, have long used color to tell one fly from another, and I suppose we always will. We can't help it: color is simply too important to be ignored in our human culture. And so last year, when I wanted to find an artificial Sulphur in my fly box, I looked around for a yellow body. It may not have meant much to the trout—I don't think it did—but it told me what I was trying to do. In this way it provided moral comfort, which is a very important feature in trout flies.

I will use yellow Sulphurs again next year, but when the fish take something low-floating and small in another color instead, I will still think that they are selective, and feel good.

Curtain, please.

Hot Creek

Michael Checchio

W<small>E FOLLOWED FLASHES OF DRY LIGHTNING</small> down into the desiccated caldera of the Owens Valley, where the mainly treeless eastern slope of the Sierra drops suddenly into tan and endless space and the sagebrush hills more closely resemble Wyoming than they do California. Here the rivers spill and disappear into the desert bottoms or the shining wastes of Nevada.

The arid basin of the Owens once was a lush valley of cattle ranches, orchards and wheat farms. But that was before Los Angeles, roughly two hundred and fifty miles away, decided to steal the water and suck this remote Eden dry. That was in the early twenties, when Los Angeles Water and Power clandestinely bought up and incorporated most of the river-bottom land and rights-of-way along the river in order to secretly irrigate crops in the San Fernando Valley and ultimately expand the metropolis. This huge rip-off of the Owens ranchers eventually became a part of the mythology of the West, where Mark Twain had earlier observed that whisky was for drinking, water for fighting over. The Owens deception also served as the inspiration for the film *Chinatown*, the *Citizen Kane* of detective movies. "You see, Mr. Gittes," John Huston's villain explains to private eye Jack Nicholson in the film's dramatic climax, "either you bring the water to L.A., or you bring L.A. to the water."

L.A. still comes to the water, but now it's to fish Hot Creek, the most carefully picked-over stream in California. Hot Creek is a tributary of the Owens River and roughly equidistant from both L.A. and my home in San Francisco. But L.A. rightly has dibs on this priceless spring creek. You see, it's the nearest decent trout fishing for any angler unlucky enough to be living in the City of Angels.

"The history of Southern California," said my friend Hal, "is nothing less than an accounting of its lost possibilities."

He spoke with the smugness all San Franciscans affect when commenting on the Southland. Here it was again: The Speech. Southern California once was a paradise of ocean, desert and freewheeling condors, where steelhead boldly swam up Malibu Creek. Whoa. Before Hal could launch into his tirade against Walt Disney and the Magic Kingdom, his right foot suddenly smashed down onto the brake of his pickup, sending the rear end of the vehicle into a series of fishtailing cosines. A jackrabbit peeled off Highway 395 unharmed.

"I hear it's good luck to hit those things," he muttered.

"Only in Reno, Hal."

It was late afternoon and the mountain shadows were absorbing the ultraviolet light. The black thunderheads had fled south toward Bishop. Hal insisted we first fish the sweeping meadow of the upper Owens River where presumably the wind wouldn't be as bad as in Hot Creek Canyon. Hal presumed wrong. The wind made the fence wires around us vibrate like plucked harpstrings and we struggled to form our casts into wind-cheating bows.

I waded into the water and felt the motion of the river slowly leave me for Lone Pine and the high desert. The lower Owens is a lost cause, siphoned off to fill the swimming pools of L.A. Well to the south, the twenty-mile-long dry bed of Owens Lake gleams like a bleached bone at the foot of the Panamints. But the upper Owens where we stood is a fly fisherman's dreamscape, one of the region's few true spring creeks. Its valley floor sits seven thousand feet above sea level in a zone of clear spring-fed headwater and perfect trout habitat. It may be the best place to stand and view the eastern wall of California. From the valley, the Sierras rise up against the sky like galleons.

The river wound languorously through the meadow; mayflies hatched and floated toward the sun. I drifted a caddis imitation over a deep cutbank and intercepted a big rainbow on its way upstream to deliver a genetic message sent an eon ago. In spring, rainbows pour out of the huge downstream impoundment of Crowley Lake to spawn. In autumn, the browns there feel the planet's pivotal tug and steam upriver just about the time mallards get the urge to rocket out of the ponds and potholes, climb to three thousand feet and point their green heads toward Mexico.

The east slope of the Sierras provides a banquet for fishermen and among anglers you will hear inevitable arguments over whether the best brown trout fishing in California is to be found in the Owens watershed or in the East Walker River just a little farther north. The case in favor of the East Walker appears largely historical now, thanks to a severe drawdown of the Bridgeport Reservoir that buried the river's spawning gravel in enough silt to fill the Astrodome. Lawsuits were filed and lawyers summoned, bearing their load of inertia. This is California, after all. Environmentalists predict a big comeback for the East Walker but Hal is not convinced. "You might as well tag the toe and close the drawer," he said.

My friend is a notorious fly-fishing misanthrope. He once showed me a scornful letter he wrote to the owners of an aquatic amusement park with the bewildering name of Marine World Africa, USA, in Vallejo, just north of San Francisco, proposing an enterprise he called "Tarpon Rodeo." Performers would ride bucking tarpon and rodeo clowns would run out and collapse into the pools to distract the giant herring. Hal assured Marine World that his idea would be more profitable than a Ponzi scheme because, as everyone knows, rodeo performers, like circus folk, "are the lowest-paid people in show business." Marine World's response, if any, was not immediately forthcoming.

Come evening, the wind stopped sweeping down the draws. We found the trunk road that leads to Hot Creek where the stream winds through a small canyon of lava outcroppings. From this narrow defile the view upstream is unmatched. The upper creek makes serpentine cuts through a stark western meadow and beyond it rise sagebrush hills and finally the black peaks of the Sierras rimed in snow. I counted nine rustic A-frames on the meadow, the housekeeping cabins of

Hot Creek Ranch. Only paying guests get to fish this stretch of open meadow. Everybody else must make do with the canyon water.

The creek here is pretty much the same as upstream: identical meadow features with a few riffles thrown in as the water gushes over cold stones and pea gravel. Underwater chara blooms and braids the currents, making long, casual drifts of the fly impossible. This calls for some of the trickiest fishing in America.

And from the look of it, this is some of the country's most intensely fished water. Fly fishermen lined up like SWAT teams along both banks of the canyon. Despite its desirability, or maybe because of it, very little of Hot Creek is actually open to the public. The canyon stretch is brief, flowing for less than a mile before hitting the warm underground discharge that gives the creek its name. The smelly, sulfurous pool that forms here makes for world-class skinny-dipping, but creates a permanent thermal barrier to the fish, blocking downstream migration to the Owens and Crowley Lake. These hot springs are here because the whole area is sunk into a huge volcanic caldera rigged with trip-wire fault lines that set off daily harmonic temblors, most too slight to actually be detected except by sensitive seismic instruments in Berkeley and Palo Alto.

There's a lot more casting room on Hot Creek Ranch if you've got the cash for a cabin. This is where the legends started, after all. This two-mile private meadow stretch is the only water in America actually restricted to fishing with dry flies, if you can believe it. Sort of like a British chalk stream with rattlesnakes. It's as if Frederic Halford had wandered confused into a Zane Grey sunset.

You're not even allowed to wade into the shallow creek for fear of crushing the delicate water plants. These effete rules were set down in 1910 when the ranch began charging anglers fifty cents a day for the privilege of casting over its huge brown trout. The dry-fly proviso was included in the covenant of sale when the ranch changed hands and remains inviolate to this day.

All these conservation measures might account for the fact that there are a staggering eleven thousand trout in every mile of this narrow little creek. Most of the Hot Creek fish are browns. The Owens, which also has private catch-and-release fishing, on the Arcularius and Alperas ranches, holds similar numbers of fish, mostly rainbows. Little wonder half of Los Angeles joined us in the valley.

For once my friend didn't make any smart-ass remarks when he saw the other anglers on the stream. Instead he proceeded to fish Hot Creek with aplomb. Hal's line looped and whistled in the air like a singing wire.

Caddises drifted by on the surface in numbers too insignificant to inspire rises. It took me a while to make out the natural camouflage of the trout hunkering down by the chara beds. But there they were, holding themselves in the current, mysterious, lovely and dumb. How many mayfly imitations do they see drift past their snouts each season? Yet somehow they never learn. Directly below me an angler lined in a fish that had fallen to his feathered booby trap. I studied the bank water at my feet for long minutes before a brown trout, well over eighteen inches, suddenly materialized in the current's cold refraction. He had been there all along. My desire to possess him was almost infernal.

Soon trout began smutting on the surface, feeding sporadically. Above the creek, clouds of tiny mayflies mated, spinning like atoms in the final light. A small rainbow grabbed my fly and performed a few aerial turns before trying to cheat me in the weeds. I brought him quickly to hand.

Nighthawks wheeled in the dusk and shadows sifted through the canyon. My big German brown made a slow-motion rise and sipped in a bug. I tied on a small fly that might have been an olive emerger, it was really too dark to tell. I cast downstream and then fed slack line out my rod tip until the tiny fly passed over the feeding lane. I repeated this three more times before the big brown rose and struck. The line sheared through the water, making a sound like a ripping bed-sheet. The fish veered erratically beneath the surface and headed for the weedbeds, but I horsed him in anyway, only a cobweb-thin leader between us.

For some moments, I held the heavy fish in my hands to admire its gigantic black spots and scattered red moons. And then I slipped the fish back into Hot Creek.

79

It's times like these, on the hike back to the pickup truck, under the first faint starlight, that you wonder just what it is you have done right with your life to deserve such a gift.

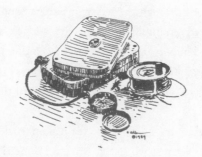

Sea-Run Cutthroats

Roderick L. Haig-Brown

MAY IS A GREAT AND GENEROUS MONTH for the trout fisherman. In the English chalk streams the fish are coming to their best and the hatching May flies drift in squadrons and flotillas and armadas, their proudly upright wings a mark that stirs both fish and fisherman. In the Adirondacks and the Catskills trout fishermen are out with the Hendrickson. Here in British Columbia the interior lakes are warm enough, but not too warm, for good fly fishing, and the great native-stock Kamloops trout come up out of Shuswap Lake to their fierce feeding on sockeye and spring salmon yearlings at Little River and off the mouth of Adams. On the coast the summer steelhead are running. In May each year I used to return to General Money his big thirteen-foot salmon rod; through the winter months it was mine because, the General said, he was too old to give it proper work to do, but by mid-May he would be thinking of early summer fish in the Stamp and would take the big rod over there to fish its easy, graceful way down the Junction Pool or the General's Pool. In May I turn to a smaller rod and go to the Island Pools to find our own run of summer fish, little fish seldom over five pounds, seldom under two, but sea-run steelhead just the same and brave fish that hit the fly hard and jump freely in the broken water. The twenty-fourth of May, a good Canadian holiday, is a day I have often celebrated with the little steelheads of the Island Pools.

The Pacific coast is great trout country. If we consider the chars as separate from trout—and I am quite certain that we should—there are in the world only three species of trout, the brown, the rainbow and the cutthroat. Of these, two are native to the Pacific coast and the slope of water west of the Rocky Mountains. This, by itself, seems to argue that the Pacific watershed has in full measure whatever it is that trout need and like; all the testing and sorting processes of evolution have left it with two trouts and given only one to all the rest of the world. The variations of environment in the watershed have developed at least two subspecies of each of these native species: the rainbow or steelhead of the coast proper becomes the Kamloops trout at medium elevations and the mountain Kamloops at high elevations; the Yellowstone cutthroat and the mountain cutthroat, as their names suggest, bear similar relationship to the coast cutthroat, the type of the species.

I suppose it is most improper to talk of degrees of nativeness. A fish or a bird or a mammal is native to a country or not native, and that is all there is to it. But for many reasons, most of them emotional and quite illogical, I feel that the cutthroat is the most native of Pacific coast game fish, just as I feel that the ruffed grouse is the most native of the continent's game birds and the cougar and the raccoon are the most native of the mammals. The cutthroat, the coast cutthroat of tidal waters particularly, is such a down-to-earth, workaday, unspectacular fish; he fits his environment so perfectly and makes such good, full use of it, following the tides and the salmon runs and the insect hatches to the limit of their yield; and he has not been, as the rainbow has, more or less successfully transplanted to all parts of the world. He lives in his own place in his own way and has his own special virtues. He is a little like the burned stumps and slash and new growth of the old logging works in that one must know and deeply love the country to appreciate him properly.

In writing of the "Game Fish of British Columbia," Professor J.R. Dymond gives an opinion of cutthroat trout that is undoubtedly shared by many anglers:

> Were it not that it (the cutthroat) occurs in the same area as two of
> the hardest fighting game fish known, its qualities would be more
> highly regarded. At times it does leap from the water when hooked,
> and often puts up quite a prolonged struggle before being landed. It

generally rises quite readily to the fly, although as a rule it takes the
fly sunk and drawn as a minnow, more readily than the dry fly.

The implication of this is that the cutthroat is not to be compared with either
the Kamloops or the steelhead as a game fish. My own opinion is that, at his best,
he is in every way comparable; and under some circumstances a discerning angler
may even find him superior.

The qualifying phrase "at his best" is important, because the cutthroat is too
often caught when he is not at his best. When the humpback fry are running in
March and April, anglers catch two- and three-pound cutthroats that are thin and
feeble after spawning. Many cutthroats are caught in low-producing lakes where
the average fish are too small to give a good account of themselves and the larger
fish are always in poor condition; and many are caught, quite unnecessarily, with
spinner and worm or other such clumsy gear and have no chance to show what
they can do. The cutthroat is at his best in a river that is open to the sea; he
should then be a short, thick fish of two pounds or more, not too long in fresh
water, with a clean white belly and a heavily spotted, green- or olive-brown back.
Such a fish will come nobly to wet fly or dry—better to the dry fly than will
Kamloops trout and far better, certainly, than steelhead—and when you set the
hook he will run as boldly as any fish of his size, and probably he will jump too.
Beyond this he has a way of his own that is fully as dangerous to tackle as the
more spectacular antics of the Kamloops, a way of boring down and out into the
heaviest stream against the lift of a fly rod and sometimes twisting his body and
shaking his head in solid, sulky strength. I have had more moments of straining
anxiety with big cutthroat trout half played out than I have with any fish, except,
perhaps, big brown trout among the weed beds and other obstructions of the
chalk streams.

The cutthroat's habit of going to sea is what makes him a really fine game fish.
There are good cutthroats and good cutthroat fishing in the cold mountain
streams that drain into the big lakes and even in ordinary landlocked rivers that
owe nothing to lake or stream; but the true sea-run cutthroat is a very special fish
and makes very special fishing. He is not truly migratory, like the steelhead and
the salmon: that is, he does not run out to sea from his river in early youth and
range freely through deep water until grown to full maturity. He is at once less
businesslike about his migration and more practical. Somewhere toward the end
of his first or second year he finds that the food available to him in fresh water is

not enough, and he simply moves downstream to find more. In tidal water or in the sea just beyond the mouth of his river he finds what he is seeking, so he stays there awhile and feeds; sometimes he moves on out as far as five or ten miles from the mouth of his river, feeding as he goes; he may even (though I am not sure of this) school with other cutthroats to feed for a while off the mouth of some stream quite distant from his own—certainly schools of big cutthroats lie at certain times off the mouths of little creeks that seem far too small to support them even as a spawning run.

But in spite of all this wandering there seems to be no sharp break between the saltwater and freshwater life of the migratory cutthroat. He may return to the fresh-water pools of his river at any time: in spring when the salmon fry hatch, in fall when the ripe salmon run, in summer when the sedge nymphs crawl thickly over the round rocks of the streambed. And he is seldom beyond reach of the fly-fisherman's search; by studying the tides and his movement in them you may catch him at his feeding in the estuary; by knowing a favorite bay or sandbar and his chosen time there you may even find him right out in salt water. In Puget Sound keen cutthroat fishermen search water as far as six or seven miles from any stream, trolling a small spinner until they hook the first fish, then changing over to the fly.

My own first meeting with sea-run cutthroats was in the Nimpkish River. I was working in a logging camp seven or eight miles away and started out for the river immediately after work on my second Saturday in camp. I took a blanket and enough food for a meal or two and promised myself a well-spent Sunday. On Saturday evening I fished one pool in the short hour or so before dark and caught three fish of about a pound. The Sunday was a bright, warm day and I started early. The Nimpkish is a broad, fine river, fast and fierce in most places, but with a few long, slow pools. On the first of these pools I wasted far too much time, but there was a strong deep run below it that spread into something less than a pool, no more, really, than a slackening in the rapid. Right in the deepest and fastest water a fine fish took, and I landed a three-pound cutthroat. At the head of the next pool was another deep, broken run, and there the second fish, a little larger than the first, came boldly to my fly. From then on I fished the fast, heavy water whenever I could find it, and by the end of the day I had four cutthroats and two rainbows, all over three pounds and one of them over four.

Since then I have caught sea-run cutthroats in the salt water, off the mouths of tiny creeks, over the tide flats of big rivers, in freshwater pools and in the brack-

ish water of shrunken river channels on the ebb tide. About ten years ago I used
to fish the mouth of the Campbell regularly with Cliff Whitaker, who was my
next-door neighbor at that time. Cliff had learned to fish and hunt in Alaska and
was a good man at both sports, aggressive and determined, a fine woodsman and
a tireless walker. He also loved human competition in hunting and fishing, which
I do not, but we found a way around that which left both of us happy and comfortable.

There are half a dozen or more good places to catch cutthroats in the tidal part
of the Campbell; two of them are sloughs, which make dull fishing; three of the
good places are best fished from a boat; and only one offers the real variations and
complications of current that one hopes for in river fishing and can, at the same
time, be fully covered by wading. On a fair run-out of tide the river breaks into a
sharp rapid just below the upper slough, and this runs for two hundred yards or
more—water where there is always a chance of picking up one or two fish on the
wet fly. At the tail of the rapid a small creek comes in, and since the creek has a
run of cohos, the cutthroats wait near its mouth when the fry are moving down.
But the best of the fishing was in a fairly big pool below the rapid. The main current of the pool swung away from the bank from which we fished and left a wide
eddy where feed collected; this was a good place. The run of current itself was
fairly good and became very good where it spread out among the short butts of
rotten piles at the tail of the pool. All this water was uncertain; on a good tide during April or May the fish were sure to come into it, but just where they would be
and how they would be feeding depended on the stage of the tide, the strength of
the river and the type of feed that was most available. The mood of the fish also
seemed to depend on just what kind of hunting they had had during the full tide
before the ebb—a fish with a really fine bellyful of sand launce or sow bugs or
sand hoppers could be a very fussy feeder when he came into the pool.

Cliff and I made a habit of going down to the pool whenever there was a good
tide, and it wasn't long before we were getting very fine results on the last two
hours of the ebb. We caught most of our fish on flies of the streamer type, tied,
not in the American way on a long single hook, but on two or three small hooks
in tandem, what the English and Scottish sea-trout fishers call "demons" or "terrors." Several Hardy patterns were very deadly: one with long dark badger hackles laid back to back, two tinsel-covered hooks and a red tag on the second hook;
another with long blue hackles, strips of light mallard and three hooks each tinsel-covered and with a red tag; a third, called the "dandy" and made up of two

hooks, mallard strips and a red hackle at the throat, was deadliest of all. But in the course of this fishing two things became evident: first, that streamer-type flies were altogether too effective under certain conditions, particularly when fish were taking freely on the last of the ebb; and second, that we were not catching fish at all well on the start of the flood, though big ones commonly moved up into the pool and began a lazy sort of feeding at that time.

Cliff and I discussed the deadliness of the streamers and agreed that we had better limit ourselves by giving up their use. At about the same time we discovered we could pick off some of the lazy feeders of the flood tide very nicely with a dry fly. From then on, all Cliff's competitive instinct was directed toward catching the fish by more and more delicate methods. We almost gave up fishing the ebb and always gave our main attention to the glassy slide of water near the piles at the tail of the pool; as soon as the tide began to slow the current there, we went down and waited for some sign of fish moving in.

They came early one day, and Cliff saw a quiet rise just behind the lowest pile. He dropped a brown and white bi-visible into the rings and hooked his fish almost as the fly touched the water; it was a three-pounder. His fly was hardly out free and dried off again when another fish rose within reach; Cliff covered him, played him and netted another three-pounder. Ten minutes later he dipped his net under a third of the same size. "That bi-visible's too deadly," he said. "Guess we'll have to quit using it."

And we did. The bi-visible we had been using was brown and white, tied on a size 9 or 10 hook. We turned to other flies on size 15 and 16 hooks and did less well with them, though still well enough. And we finally went one stage farther still, to upstream nymph fishing with flies as small as size 17. The nymphs were more attractive to the fish than were the small dry flies, but the fishing was actually more exciting and more difficult, because light and water conditions made it hard to tell when a fish had taken the nymphs; we were usually wading deep and looking toward the sun across smooth water whose reflecting surface concealed the faint flash of a moving fish that the nymph-fisherman generally depends on.

That seems to show that you can go to almost any refinement of fly-fishing and still find sea-run cutthroats willing to meet you halfway. But in spite of the sport they give in tidal waters, I still prefer to catch them when they have left the estuaries of the freshwater pools. Tidal waters can be very beautiful. I remember an evening below the falls of Theimar Creek, when the sunset light was blood red on the shiny wet sand of the tide flats and big cutthroats were rising in the narrow channel all down the length of a seaweed-covered log. I remember an August sunrise in the mouth of the Campbell, off the point of the Spit, when big cutthroats in perfect condition came to our flies so fast and hard that we each had a limit within an hour or two; outside the tyee fishermen were passing up and down in their white rowboats, and a little westerly wind came up to scuff the water of Discovery Passage as the full daylight made it blue; behind us the mountains of Vancouver Island were black and white with rock and snow, and across from us the Coast Range was jagged and tall and endless from farthest south to farthest north. Those were good times. But in the comings and goings of the cutthroats in fresh water there is something more than good fishing, something more than any simple beauty of surroundings. Each movement is an outward sign of a change in the year's cycle; more than a sign, it is an actual part of both change and cycle. And knowledge of the movements in any particular river is the seal of one's intimacy with the country at least as much as it is a test of one's knowledge as a fisherman.

In March and April and on into May the cutthroats are there because the salmon fry are coming up from the gravel and moving down; the fishing is often quick and fierce, with a big wet fly quickly cast to a slashing rise and worked back fast. Fish show in unexpected places, in short eddies behind rocks in the rapids, off the mouths of little creeks, and in all the expected places as well. Sometimes the May flies hatch thickly, and not a trout will stir to a wet fly, though fish after fish will come to a dry blue quill or a little iron blue. Then on some hot day in May, the big black ants put out their wings and make their brief mating flight; for a day, or perhaps two days, the river is full of drowned or drowning ants, and the fish feed on them and come to a dry fly that is not too tidily tied and not too well greased, something bedraggled and half-drowned like the ants themselves. After that there is a change, and there seem few cutthroats in the freshwater pools of the Campbell. I used to say of June and July: it's hardly worth going up—there won't be any fish. But the days are so good and the river is so bright that one goes sometimes just for the pleasure of being out in the sun and the summer, with running water all about one and the trees green on the banks.

I have been surprised so many times now that I am careful what I say about June and July. It was a June afternoon that I went up to the head of the Sandy Pool, lay on the beach for a while in the sun and at last walked lazily down into the

87

water to make a few casts before going home. Just as soon as my fly reached out into the fast water a trout took hold, a good trout, short and thick and over two pounds. I went on fishing and soon hooked a second fish, the most beautiful cut-throat, I think, that I have ever hooked; he was a two-pounder, like the first one, but shorter still and thicker, splendidly marked with a rich pattern of heavy spots all over the deep and shining green of his back and sides. That was all for that afternoon, but it was enough to leave the short June hour as clear and sharp in my memory as any fishing time.

Two years ago a July day looked good, and I went to the Island Pools, just to look them over. I told myself that the fish wouldn't come in for a couple of weeks yet. So I worked along the bar and floated a Mackenzie River bucktail down the runs, dancing it back to me from wave top to wave top on the upstream wind, low-ering my rod to slack the line and let the fly ride the rough water down again. It seldom finished the ride. The big cutthroats, three-pounders, some of them nearly four pounds, came at it like fiercer creatures than any fish, leapt right out of the water with it, fought me for possession of it and yielded only to utter exhaustion and the lift of the net.

So I have no wisdom that will let me write of June and July, even in my own river that I know well. And the wisdom I once had for August and September is shaken a little and likely to grow shakier yet as I grow older and learn to watch more closely. Sometimes in the second week of August the humpback salmon run into the river. With them, I used to say, come the big cutthroats that are matur-ing to spawn in the following February—magnificent fish that have attained their full weight and strength and a cunning or dourness that makes them hard to catch on bright August days in the Canyon Pool. I argued that they came into the river because of their maturity, following the maturity of the humpbacks rather than in any hope of feeding on salmon eggs that would not be dropped to the gravel for another two months. It was a nice theory, but in the last two or three years I've noticed the cutthroats before the humpbacks. I asked General Money about that, and he had noticed the same thing. So I no longer know why they come in then— I only know that I try to get away to the Canyon Pool as soon as I can after the first of August.

That August fishing in the Canyon Pool is the finest cutthroat fishing I have had anywhere. The fish are very big—I have killed several that weighed within an ounce of four pounds and have lost some that I know were over five pounds—and they can be superlatively difficult. They are not feeding, for only very rarely is there so much as a May-fly nymph in a stomach; they lie in water six or eight feet deep, unrippled by the slightest stir of wind and burnished by the full glare of summer sun. When they rise, they come right up from the bottom, and every cast that covers them is a really long cast. When they feel the hook, they turn and run with a pull that makes every one seem a ten-pounder, and at the end of that first long run, well down at the tail of the pool, they jump with a coho's wildness. That part is easy. Coaxing them back up the pool again, trying to keep them from disturbing the rest of the water, meeting their plunging, boring, heavy resistance and yielding no more than must be yielded to save 2X gut is the hard part, the part that makes fingers clumsy and trembling and the heart quick in the chest when it's time to reach for the net.

After August you may perhaps find cutthroats again in October, when the cohos run up on the first heavy fall rains. They seem less important then, because their season is almost over and you're fishing a big fly and heavy gut for the cohos anyway—tackle too clumsy for a trout—so you turn them back to live and spawn. And again in steelhead time, in December and January and February, they are there, heavy with spawn now, dark, with red gill covers and golden bellies. I hold them hard and bring them in fast, then reach down for the shank of the hook and twist the barb quickly away from them so that they can go back without harm to their important affairs. But recently a few big cutthroats have been caught and killed as steelheads in the Campbell. I saw one two seasons ago that weighed six and a half pounds. This season there was one that weighed well over seven pounds. I hope that next August, or one August soon, in the Canyon Pool . . .

Big Water

John Engels

My BROTHER AND I never caught
one of the big rainbows for which the Soo
was famous, though he hooked into something once
that smashed his rod with one run,
and left him swearing
like a sonuvabitch. Oh it was exciting
just to know they were there, the big fish,
and when the water was low

and the light was right you could look down
from the top of the dam at the head
of the river and see them, long
gray shapes lying easy in the water,
almost still, maybe once in a while
a little curl of a fin. One year
we heard a local had been arrested
with a thirty-three pounder

that he'd speared. That kept us coming back
five years more at least, though between us
we caught exactly nothing, *half*
of nothing apiece, my brother said,
and we worked hard for it. We'd cross the locks
and fish all day in the tail race below

the powerhouse, edging out into
the heavy water to where
we didn't dare take another step, or turn
around even, and had to back
into shore over stones round and smooth
and slippery as you'd imagine
skull bones might be. Or we'd fish

from the spit of land beyond the tail race, in the rapids, bells
ringing behind us, horns bellowing and whistles screaming
from the ore carriers warped in to the big bollards
on the locks, men in foreign-looking caps
yelling up messages
to the crews on deck: *If you see Georgie McInnis*
in Duluth, tell him Oley
is working at the Soo. Other men

on the approaches to the locks
fished for whitefish with forty feet of line, and two
large mayflies on the hook, and you could look down
and see shining schools of fry, thirty yards
across, and suddenly
they'd melt away as a big trout
came cruising by only ten
or twelve feet down. It was good times, that's for sure,

when my brother and I
could get together at the Soo, big trout
on our minds, we'd be together at the Soo,
where we stayed at Mrs. Letourneau's Boarding House
every year in August for fourteen years

because it was cheap, and there was a tub
set on lion paws, and long enough
for a tall man to straighten out his legs, and deep enough
to bring the water to his chest—stayed there
in spite of the bugs. I remember
the first night there, I dreamed
I was covered with specks
of fire, woke up, there was a bug
working on me, I jumped up and pulled
the covers off the mattress, there they were,
half a dozen things big as potato bugs crawling up
the bed board, and I woke up my brother

in a panic, I said "There's bedbugs, the place
is crawling with bugs," but in the war he'd served
in India with the Brits, with kraits and cobras and bugs
that could swell your balls
to the size of cantaloupes, "What of it,
go to sleep!" he said. So what the hell, I went out
to the car and spent the night
in the back seat. Every year for fourteen years

my brother and I went back to work
the rapids, our heads aching with what
it would be like to hang into one
of those fish. Never did. Last year I went
back to the Soo alone, stayed one day, first time

in years, everything changed, my brother
dead, wife and daughter
dead, nobody talking

about big fish, the whitefish
long gone account of the lampreys, likewise
the lakers, everybody's mind
on something else or other, though lots
of guys out fishing on the docks
because of not much work,

and nothing much else to do, sitting there
waiting it out, bored and cold

in a sheeting rain that day, water pouring
off their hats and down their necks and into the sleeves
of their jackets every time they raised
their arms, and to top it off
the day I was there the turbines
were shut down, and the slots closed, the race
no more than a series of riffles and runs
between pools—though in the taverns

the proof was there, up on the walls behind the bars, over the mirrors,
in glass cases, there they were, the big fish, some of them
a little the worse for the years
they'd hung there, dusty, varnish peeling, paint
pretty garish in some cases, nevertheless for all
the bug-eyes, cracked and missing fins
there they were, mounts

of twelve- and fifteen-pound rainbows
came to the fly out there
in the rapids, the guides
straining at their poles trying to hold the canoes
upright and steady, the canoes
still pitching and rolling plenty, the sports
rolling out their heavy lines, the flies
floating down the feeding lanes
of that demented water,

and the great trout coming
to the fly, breaking water, suspending themselves
over the rapids, an outburst, a levitation
of high-leaping rainbows, striped scarlet, striped
cherry-red, green-
gilled, brilliant
in the ripe, sun-smelling day!

Karen's Pool

Harry Middleton

To the old men, Starlight Creek was more than water and trout, more than fishing; it was life itself, immediate, volatile and vital, and they were singularly devoted to it and its well-being and to the trout that lived in its cold waters. The creek, the valley it flowed through, and the high country it seeped down from provided whatever spiritual nourishment they needed. There is nothing like a swift, cold trout stream to clear a man's head, raise his temperature and blood pressure. No matter where we were on the place, we could always hear the creek on the wind, the mollifying sound of rushing water, a generous palliative, freely given.

Albert and Emerson were strict monogamists, devoted solely to the trout in Starlight Creek. The trout, mostly rainbows, were not all that big or spectacular, as trout go. Indeed, they weren't even native trout. They were western trout that had been stocked in the mountains beginning in the 1940s after the big dam projects in the region changed the nature of so many of northwestern Arkansas' streams, transforming them from warm-water bass rivers to cold-water trout habitat. All this mattered little. All that mattered to Albert and Emerson was that there were trout. Being bachelors, though, allowed for some lapses of fidelity, especially in the early summer when they would spend weeks along Susan's Branch casting their fly lines into the warmer water, hoping to get the attention of the stream's abundant but spooky population of smallmouth bass. And then they would come back, as always, to Starlight Creek, for as much as they admired the beauty and fight of the smallmouth bass, it wasn't a trout.

Trout did not simply fascinate the old men; they obsessed them. Everything about trout perplexed and delighted them. Any creature so graceful, powerful, and secretive, so unwilling to adapt to civilization, was a creature worthy of respect. And trout were such likable fish: recalcitrant, intractable, defiant. Everything spooked them, sent them swimming for cover, for survival.

"They're doomed," said Albert one afternoon as we sat on the big flat stone by the river birch at the edge of Karen's Pool.

"Who is?" I asked, somewhat startled because Albert rarely talked while he was on the creek and even when he did speak, it was never about angling.

"Trout," he said, his voice low and sullen. "Bring civilization within a mile of them and they turn belly up. It's wildness for them or nothing. No compromises. They believe in the simple life. Cold water, plenty of food, and clean oxygen. Wildness. Dumb bastards don't know any better, I guess." He took another bite of his egg sandwich and a long pull of cool creek water and shook his head. "Doomed. Poor dumb bastards. Doomed, and me along with them, thank whatever gods there are."

There was nothing snobbish about the old men's affinity for trout. They were drawn to trout and the fly rod not out of any need to be among the sophisticated anglers associated with the sport, but rather to associate more fully with trout. Trout appealed to Emerson and Albert because trout seemed to lead a life as precarious as their own, awkwardly balanced on the edge of extinction, the complete emptiness of oblivion. Too, they admired the trout's wariness, its unwavering suspicion that something was out to get it, to do it in. The trout had gotten to be such an ancient fish, they believed, because of its prudence. Trout trusted nothing, not even other trout. All they knew vibrated in their instinct, their primordial blood. All of these qualities intrigued Albert and Emerson. Such wildness captivated them, drew them irresistibly into the waters of Starlight Creek, fly rod in hand, an act, an effort, however feeble, to immerse themselves in the trout's world.

The hold trout had on them and ultimately on me was nearly absolute, like a spell, some kind of vexing yet delightful piscine voodoo. Trout simply cannot be figured out, no matter how much technology they are exposed to or bombarded with. Trout are steadfastly ornery and beyond reform, and the old men admired, even envied, their unyielding tenacity.

Such a fish demanded, of course, special attention, certain considerations, a method of pursuit as finicky and fastidious as their own behavior. A curious fish insists on a curious form of angling, one heavy with respect, tradition, skill, and challenge. If there was only one fish in the lives of Albert and Emerson, Elias Wonder, and soon me, so was there only one correct way to fish for it—with the fly rod. And not just any fly rod, but a subtle, willowy, handmade bamboo fly rod, a good line, a trustworthy reel, tippets as delicate as gossamer, and the smallest dry flies possible. Albert and Emerson had no spare time for hobbies or sports or insignificant moments of recreation. To them fly fishing transcended all of these pastimes. It was a personal and private act of faith between angler, stream, and trout. Fly fishing did not come to these two poor subsistence farmers as a right of birth, but as a blessing in what was an otherwise hard and often despairing life. Consequently, what little theology they held to rested firmly in the waters of Starlight Creek and the trout that struggled there for survival. Indeed, as Albert said on more than one silver-gray morning before daylight took hold, trout and streams and lithe bamboo rods were as close to the divine as he and Emerson and Elias Wonder, that irascible malcontent, were likely to come. Starlight Creek whispered the gospel, the good news, loud and clear, and every trout that rose to their flies was an unforgettable sermon of color and motion, resolve and urgency, grace and the elusiveness of life in the present where it throbbed with such compelling and enthralling power. Standing in the waters of Karen's Pool, the old men worked the supple bamboo rods, limber as relaxed muscle, and waited for the trout to rise and draw them to what was a nearer and more immediate, more accessible, more forgiving heaven.

97

Fly fishing absorbed them, touched every aspect of their lives on and off the creek. To say that it was all just a matter of catching fish would be like saying that astronomy is nothing more than noticing the stars. Fly fishing, like the noble trout, had character, a tough eloquence about it. Despite the simplicity of its mechanics, it demanded that the angler become truly involved with trout, even get in the water with them, become, if only temporarily, part of their ancient and wild lives. Once an angler took up the fly rod, he became heir to a sturdy body of opinion, belief, and notions, all of which tended to bind the angler, the fly rod and trout together for a lifetime. Albert and Emerson had fished with the fly rod for more than sixty years and never tired of its magic, never stopped seeking its untouched potential. Fly rods in hand, they entered into the natural world, a world of risk, chance, raw energy, adventure.

Given the erratic nature of trout, it seemed somehow fitting to Albert and Emerson that fly fishing should employ as its chief implement a humble little rod made of bamboo. Yet it is a deadly instrument, as lethal and efficient in the hands of a trout fisherman as a sharpened ax is in the hands of a lumberjack. The fly rod is at best a curious thing, fitful, moody, chameleon-like. Depending on the skill of the angler, handling the bamboo rod can be as simple and effortless as knotting a tie or as complex as brain surgery. Whatever an angler's skill, the fly rod is an outstanding companion, a welcome conversationalist because it speaks not in words but in motion and energy.

No one at Trail's End, not Emerson, Albert, Elias Wonder, or me, fit the image of the dapper, genteel, sophisticated fly fisherman who frequents the outdoor catalogs and so much of outdoor literature. We hadn't a tweed coat among us or a wicker creel or a handsome Leonard or Payne rod. The old men believed earnestly that the principal ingredient of fly fishing was a good sense of humor, while avoiding anything that smacked of pretense, technology, or just plain foolishness.

Albert and Emerson owned many fly rods during their lifetimes, but admired none so much as the bamboo rod, which was the rod of their youth. It was the only rod they truly trusted, a rod not yet burdened with the false reputation of being a flimsy and expensive artifact, a plaything of the rich, something to collect rather than use.

By the 1960s technology had come to fly fishing and there were new rods appearing, made of fiberglass, fast rods, powerful rods. Albert tried one not long before he died. He wiggled it in Bates's store a few times, a frown on his face, his motions stiff, forced. The rod was nine feet long and threw a 6-weight forward line. Again he wiggled it, then cast the line through the entire length of the store and into the street beyond. He set it down. "I just don't feel it," he said. Again, he looked at the big, imposing rod, shook his head glumly. "Don't feel anything, really, except a kind of cold, clammy feeling."

I touched the rod, studied it closely, thought of the beautiful cast Albert had made with it. Why, the line must have traveled at least one hundred feet. To me the rod seemed a thing of great power and even greater temptation. I nudged the old man and asked, "What don't you feel, Albert?"

"Trout," said Albert abruptly, a tinge of disappointment in his voice, as though he had expected that I would grasp the rod's failings as quickly and surely as he had. "That subtle finesse that will put a No. 18 dry fly on a quarter at forty feet. This rod is all right, I suppose. It's got power, but power alone won't catch trout. I'll stay with bamboo. It has grace, a soothing touch."

Unlike the new glass rods, bamboo rods demanded regular attention and care. There developed over time a loyal bond between the bamboo rod and the angler as one ultimately became the extension of the other. All those long days and cool evenings sitting by the creek watching the old men fish, I knew that with each cast there was also a building sense of excitement and exhilaration because they believed that in hooking a trout the hook not only brought the fish to them but drug them deeper into the trout's element, the remnant wilderness that surrounded them.

The old men collected fly rods the way small boys collect marbles or baseball cards. Emerson had ten rods. He looked after them as though they were his children. Even cleaning them in the evening boosted his spirits. He and Albert never considered bamboo rods as things. No, they were the inanimate creeping toward life, wands as full of excitement, chance, fortune and agony as the natural world. Supple, malleable, like the passage of life itself, something capable of giving without ever giving up or giving way. Albert owned three good rods and two reels. The workshop off the kitchen held the usual assortment of leaders, lines, hooks, tippet material, waders, dry flies, wet flies, and nymphs, all of which they had either made or smuggled into Oglala County from the outdoor catalog companies by mail. Not much really, when you consider they were up against trout. It was their desire to keep angling a simple art and therefore they aspired to put as little technical wizardry between them and the trout as possible.

While the old men fished every day, through every season, they kept few trout. Trout were too special, too precious a part of the natural world to kill. Releasing them back into the cool waters of the creek unharmed stood as the central axiom of their angling epistemology. They clung to the notion, whether true or not, that once released, left to live, a trout became that rarest of possibilities—a part of the natural world that might, with luck, be experienced more than once, a wonder that could go on to reproduce itself, keep populating the creek's inexorable and delightful chaos, its ever-present portrait of life.

So, to Albert and Emerson and Elias Wonder, fly fishing seemed life's most reassuring constant. It got them out of the fields, away from the house, put them into the creek's waters, let them feel that perpetual tug against their flesh, the measure of life immediate, real, and deep, and it put them, sometimes, eye to eye with the vigor and intensity and elegance of trout.

99

Often, as I watched from beside the river birch, every cast seemed to me almost purposely designed to slow time, to suspend the present moment for as long as possible. Only the creek mattered and the presentation of the fly, how it behaved on the water, and the way the light came off the surface of the creek in bursts of orange and yellow and white, and how good the wind felt on my face, and the cold water numbing your calves and thighs, and, always, the wary trout. This was what mattered—not yesterday, not even tomorrow, not last year or anything from the past, which the old men refused to be shackled to as fiercely as they avoided being haunted by any vision or portent of what seemed to be a troubled future. What mattered was the momentary certainty of the hills, Starlight Creek, and trout. After that, all they were sure of was that their continued existence, like that of the trout, was a matter of considerable doubt.

The intricacies of fly fishing intrigued and fascinated the old men. After all, the serious fly fisherman had to depend as much on his skill and intelligence as on blind luck. The way Emerson saw it, fly fishing had saved them from the dreary life of subsistence farmers, given them a way to participate in the rhythms of the natural world other than by shouldering a hoe. Too, fly fishing was great therapy. It kept them nearly sane, out of trouble, usually sober, and allowed them to pursue a life that, in imagination at least, had no limits or boundaries.

For as long as I knew them, they never worried once about actually landing a fish. Like every seasoned trout angler, they knew they were, in the end, no match for trout. The contest was unfair from the start: the trout held all the aces. Curiously, it was a comfort to them that they would never get the best of Starlight Creek or its uncanny trout. The challenge never dulled; the thrill never faded. The reward was angling itself, just meeting the trout in its world, on its own terms, feeling the tenuous nature of its life and suddenly understanding the tenuousness of your own.

Of the trout's many excellent qualities, it was its uncompromising refusal to accept the world on man's conditions that enticed Albert and Emerson, lured them to Starlight Creek day after day. How they doted on the trout's piscatorial petulance. No other fish they knew was as irascible, churlish, disagreeable, temperamental, or provocative, loyal only to its own survival. Elias Wonder's passion went deeper still. Like him, trout seemed to have a bilious, splenetic attitude toward life, and a man could experience no greater satisfaction than pursuing an ancient fish that just didn't give a damn about anything but itself. It seemed a puzzling relationship. Trout fishermen revere the trout; trout, on the other hand, unaware of their sublime standing in man's world, revere nothing, including man, a creature they seem to view with special contempt. Nihilism is a rare trait in fish but trout are full of it. The old men liked that. Trout were estimable companions, saying not a word, but speaking instead in motions, wrinkles of water, mystery and surprise.

Whenever I watched the old men on the creek, a feeling, odd yet comforting, swept over me like a chill that settled in my spine and spread, touching every nerve, a feeling that I was witnessing a poignant, intensely private drama, a catechism of life, tension and resolution, played out in an intimate struggle between man and trout. A passion play, a mystery, an extravagance, a morality play, a telling tableau, all of these at once as each of the old men cast, trying not so much to hook a trout as to immerse himself in the trout's wildness.

On a day in March, Albert got up before daybreak and, as usual, took his rod and walked down the worn path to the creek. He walked downstream and stopped finally at Cody's Rock, where he knew there were some fine trout and a mammoth grizzled brown with a scarred lip that he had been trying to catch since October. Albert fished for hours. He moaned, said his luck had gone sour. He waded out of the creek, his patched, faded waders looking shiny as ebony, and sat on the big rock. He began wiping the moisture off his rod, a $7\frac{1}{2}$-foot two-piece Phillipson that was as smooth and dark as wild cherry bark and as limber as a length of willow. He began to talk, which was unlike him. All his life Albert had been a man who liked angling for trout more than he liked talking about trout.

"A good rod," he said, laying the Phillipson across his lap. "Hooked into many a dream with it." In a soft voice he told me he liked fly fishing because it had backbone and character. It was a noble way of life. And if fly fishing provided the angler with humbling doses of misery and disappointment, so too did it yield adventure, elation, glorious isolation enough to ease a man's troubled heart. He figured he had cast a line for sixty years at least and still it thrilled him, filled him with expectation, drained away the tedium of the farm like pus from a wound. He found it hard to put his feelings into words. "It's more than excitement," he said, looking out over the creek, down into its clear, clean water. "It's more like an alliance of enchantment and exuberance, a pleasing delirium that at last distills down into a sense of real peace, absolute and perfect." He turned back to me, laughing. "God, that was a mouthful of rambling mush. I need to take a course. My language is too prolix. But I hope you get the core of what I'm saying about angling." I nodded and returned his smile.

He stood at the edge of Cody's Rock and cast again, letting the fly rest upstream, about midway in the current. I found myself thinking that each cast carried with it not only the hope of a trout on the rise, but a sense of renewal as well. He cast again and I could tell from his eyes that he was deep in concentration and that the rod was an extension of his emotions, as real and genuine as any he had ever experienced, including love, which he had embraced and lost five times over. Later that morning, he confided in me that trout anglers overcame their misfortunes by developing selective memories, a portion of the mind where all the good days, all the good trout water, the good rods, the good trout, were stored, ready to surge through every cell and muscle, a rejuvenation of body and spirit. And then Albert took a hard-boiled egg from his coat pocket, peeled it, and put the shell back into his pocket. He ate it leaning up against Cody's Rock, staring at the day's fading light coming off the creek in clouds of soft yellow vapor.

After fishing nearly all day around Cody's Rock, I walked upstream to Karen's Pool, and saw Emerson fishing there along with Elias Wonder, who stood on the far side of the pool. I took my usual seat up against the birch tree, took long gulps of warm root beer from my canteen. I remember thinking on that late afternoon that the great lure of fly fishing is that it is more of a journey than a quest, a journey with unlimited beginnings and no definitive end. The angler hopes for nothing and prays for everything; he expects nothing and accepts all that comes his way. And although he knows all along that he will never sink his hook into a trout stream's true mystery, the desire to try, to cast once more and once more again, is never quenched, for there is always that chance that one more cast will carry him beyond skill and luck and bring him untarnished magic.

For me, there was never any question that some kind of magic mingled with the waters of Starlight Creek. Sometimes as I fished the creek at dusk when the light came off the water soft as velvet and blue shadows lengthened in the woods, I would suddenly feel lightheaded, dizzy, for an instant having no more substance than a cloud of cool mist on the stream. A cleansing feeling, beyond fear or confusion. For that moment the world around me was sensible and full of purpose, soaked in reason and resignation. A boy's clumsy attempt to dismantle himself into the elements, a pool of molecules mingling with the creek and the air, the light overhead, the trout deep in the cold, translucent water. Of course, it never happened, but I never doubted that it could, for I knew that where there was cold trout water there was hope, of a kind.

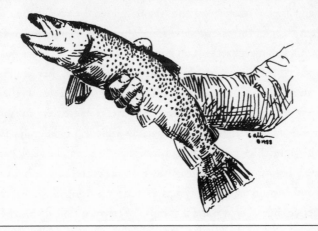

Midstream

Thomas McGuane

IN OCTOBER, I looked off the wooden bridge and into the small river I had
come to like so well. It was nearly covered with yellow cottonwood leaves; they
diagrammed its currents as they swept toward each other around the framework
of the old boxcar out of which the bridge was made. A cold wind eddied down the
river into my face, and I was ready to decide that to everything there is a season
and that trout season was over. Fall gives us a vague feeling that the end of everything is at hand; here I felt that when the snow melted in the spring my wonderful little river would be gone.

I don't know if it was literally the first time I saw that river, but it is the first
time I remember seeing it. I came down the side of the basin riding a young mare.
I could see, first, the tree line of the small river, then, here and there, flashes of its
runs and pools as it made its way through the pastureland of its own small valley.
There were a few bright and geometric lines where irrigation ditches made diago-
nals from its more eloquent meanders, and a few small flooded areas where the
water had stopped to reflect the clouds and the sky. It was a river with an indif-
ferent fishing reputation.

Young anglers love new rivers the way they love the rest of their lives. Time doesn't seem to be of the essence and somewhere in the system is what they are looking for. Older anglers set foot on streams the location of whose pools is as yet unknown with a trace of inertia. Like sentimental drunks, they are interested in what they already know. Yet soon enough, any river reminds us of others, and the logic of a new one is a revelation. It's the pools and runs we have already seen that help us uncode the holding water: the shallow riffle is a buildup for the cobbled channel where the thick trout nymph with mirror flashes; the slack back channel with the leafy bottom is not just frog water but a faithful reservoir for the joyous brook beyond. An undisturbed river is as perfect a thing as we will ever know, every refractive slide of cold water a glimpse of eternity.

The first evening I fished the river, I walked through a meadow that lay at the bottom of a curved red cliff, a swerving curve with a close-grained mantle of sage and prairie grasses. It could be that the river cut that curve, then wandered a quarter-mile south; but there you have it, the narrow shining band, the red curve, and the prairie. As I sauntered along with my fly rod, hope began to build in the perceived glamour of my condition: a deep breath.

"Ah."

There was a stand of mature aspens with hard white trunks on the edge of meadow and next to the water. The grass was knee deep. White summer clouds towered without motion. Once I had crossed to that spot, I could make out the progress of small animals, fanning away from my approach. I hurried forward in an attempt to see what they were, and a young raccoon shot up one of the slick aspens, then, losing traction, made a slow, baffled descent back into the grass. By shuffling around, I managed to have four of them either going up or sliding down at once. They were about a foot tall, and something about their matching size and identical bandit masks, coupled with their misjudgment of aspens as escape routes, gave me a sense of real glee at the originality of things. The new river gurgled in the bank.

I walked in and felt its pull against my legs. Current is a mysterious thing. It is the motion of the river leaving us, and it is as curious and thrilling a thing as a distant train at night. The waters of this new river, pouring from high in a Montana wilderness, are bound for the Gulf of Mexico. The idea that so much as a single molecule of the rushing chute before me was headed for Tampico was as eerie as the moon throwing a salty flood over the tidelands and then retrieving it. Things that pass us, go somewhere else, and don't come back seem to communicate directly with the soul. That the fisherman plies his craft on the surface of such a thing possibly accounts for his contemplative nature.

I once thought that this was somehow not true of aircraft, that they were too new and lacked mystery. But I lived for a time in the mountainous path of B-52 nighttime traffic. The faraway thunder that rose and fell to the west had the same quality of distance and departure that trains and rivers have. One pale summer night, I made out the darkened shape of one of these death ships against the stars, and shivered to think of the freshness of the high prairie where I was living beneath that great bird and its eggs of destruction.

The only bird today was a little water dipper, one of those ouzel-like nervous wrecks that seem not to differentiate between air and water, and stroll through both with aplomb. I associate them with some half-serious elfin twilight, a thing which, like the raccoons, suggests that there is a playful element in creation. I began to feel the animal focus that a river brings on as you unravel the current in search of holding water.

The learning of this river corresponded with the waning of runoff. My casting arm was still cold from winter, and I waded like a spavined donkey. I am always careful to go as light as possible early on, knowing that any little thing will throw me off; and the matter of getting over round, slick rocks, judging the depth and speed of current—things like these start out tough. One feels timid. Later in the year, you make the long, downstream pirouettes in deep fast water that you'd never chance when you're rusty.

It is a matter of ceremony to get rid of stuff. The winter has usually made me yield to some dubious gadgets, and you're at war with such things if the main idea of fishing is to be preserved. The net can go. It snags in brush and catches fly line. If it is properly out of the way, you can't get at it when you need it. Landing fish without a net adds to the trick and makes the whole thing better. Make it one box of flies. I tried to stick to this and ended up buying the king of Wheatlies, a double-sided brute that allows me to cheat on the single-box system. No monofilament clippers. Teeth work great. Trifles like leader sink, flyline cleaner, and geegaws that help you tie knots must go. You may bring the hemostat, because to pinch down barbs and make quick, clean releases of the fabled trout help everything else make sense. Bring a normal rod, with a five- or six-weight line, because in early season the handle you have on hatches is not yet sufficient and you must be prepared to range through maybe eight fly sizes. Weird rod weights reflect armchair fantasies and often produce chagrin on the water.

I began to have a look at the river. It went through hard ground but cut deep. It was like a scribe line at the base of sine and cosine curves of bank banded at the top with a thin layer of topsoil. The river bottom was entirely rocks, small rounded ones, and on either side were the plateaus of similar stones, representing the water levels of thousands of previous years. A few mayflies drifted past in insignificant numbers. I understand that mayflies bear a rather antique genetic code themselves, expressed in size and color, and my hope is that if things pick up, I have the right imitations in my box.

As I face new water, I always ask myself if I am going to fish with a nymph or not. Presumably, you do not walk straight into rising trout. Camus said that the only serious question is whether or not to commit suicide. This is rather like the nymph question. It takes weight, a weighted fly, split shot. Casting becomes a matter of spitting this mess out and being orderly about it. It requires a higher order of streamcraft than any other kind of fishing, because it truly calls upon the angler to see the river in all its dimensions. Gone are the joys of casting, the steady meter and adjustment of loop that compare to walking or rowing. The joys of casting are gone because this ignoble outfit has ruined the action of your fly rod.

Still, you must show purpose. American shame at leisure has produced the latest no-nonsense stance in sport, the "streamside entomologist" and the "head-hunter" being the most appalling instances that come readily to mind. No longer sufficiently human to contemplate the relationship of life to eternity, the glandular modern sport worries whether or not he is wasting time. Small towns used to have a mock-notorious character who didn't feel this way, the mythical individual who hung the GONE FISHIN' sign in the window of his establishment. We often made him a barber or someone remote from life-and-death matters. Sometimes we let him be a country doctor, and it was very rakish to drift grubs in a farm pond against the possible background of breech birth or peritonitis. Finally, we took it as very American to stand up and be superfluous in the glaring light of Manifest Destiny.

In the shock and delight of new water, my thoughts were entirely ineffective. What is the relationship of the bottom to the water, to the landscape through which it flows, to the life of the air around it all and the vegetation that alters the wind and interferes with the light? In other words, should one fish that deep outer bank—shaded by a hedge of wild junipers—with a nymph, or would it be better to imitate the few pale morning duns that are drifting around but not yet inspiring any surface feeding? In the latter case, that glassy run below the pool is the spot. For a moment, I avoid the conundrum by turning into another river object, a man-

like thing with the unmoving fly rod. Because time has stopped, I really don't concern myself with an eager companion who has already put three on the beach.

Mortality being what it is, any new river could be your last. This charmless notion runs very deep in us and does produce, besides the tightening around the mouth, a sweet and consoling inventory of all the previous rivers in your life. Finally, the fit is so perfect that it gives the illusion that there is but one river, a Platonic gem. There are more variations within any one good river than there are between a number of good rivers. I have been fortunate in that my life-river has a few steelhead in the lower reaches, as well as Oregon harvest trout and the sea-run browns of Ireland; there are Michigan brook trout in the deep bends, braided channels in hundred-mile sections from the Missouri headwaters trout theme park; and here and there are the see-through pools of New Zealand. Fire and water unlock the mind to a kind of mental zero gravity in which resemblances drift toward one another. The trout fisherman finishes his life with but one river.

All this is getting fairly far-fetched; still, like the trout, we must find a way of moving through water with the least amount of displacement. The more we fish, the more weightlessly and quietly we move through a river and among its fish, and the more we resemble our own minds in the bliss of angling.

I came to a pool where a tree with numerous branches had fallen. Its leaves were long gone, and the branches tugged lightly in the slight current that went through the pool. A remarkable thing was happening: a good-size brown was jumping among the lowest branches, clearly knocking insects loose to eat. Every three or four minutes it vaulted into the brush over its window and fell back into the water. I knew if I could get any kind of a float, I would have a solid taker. I looked at all the angles, and the only idea I could come up with was that it was a good time to light a cigar. In a moment, the excellent smoke of Honduras rose through the cottonwoods. I waited for an idea to form, a solution, but it never happened. In the end, I reared back and fired a size 14 Henryville Caddis into the brush. It wound around a twig and hung in midair. The trout didn't jump at it suicidally. I didn't get the fly back.

Angling doesn't turn on stunts. The steady movements of the habituated gatherer produce the harvest. This of course must be in the service of some real stream knowledge. But some fishing, especially for sea-run fish, rewards a robotic capacity for replicating casts, piling up the repetitions until the strike is induced.

The river made an angular move to the south into the faraway smoky hills. In the bend, there was some workmanlike dry-wall riprap that must have reflected the Scandinavian local heritage. The usual western approach would be to roll an old car into the river at the point of erosion. Instead of that, I found neatly laid cobbles that gave the impression that the river was slowly revealing an archaeological enigma or the foundations of a church. But for the next forty yards, the clear water trembled deep and steady over a mottled bottom, and I took three hearty browns that flung themselves upon the bright surface of the run. When I was young and in the thrall of religion, I used to imagine various bands of angels, which were differentiated principally by size. The smallest ones were under a foot in height, silvery and rapid, and able to move in any plane at will. The three trout in that run reminded me of those imaginary beings.

The river lay down at the bottom of a pencil-thin valley, and though I could see the wind in the tops of the trees, I could barely feel it where I fished. The casts stretched out and probed without unwarranted shepherd's crooks, blowbacks, or tippet puddles. I came to a favorite kind of stretch: 20 or 30 yards of very shallow riffle with a deep green slot on the outside curve. In this kind of conformation, you wade in thin, fast water easily and feel a bit of elevation to your quarry. The slot seemed to drain a large oxygenated area, and it was the only good holding water around. Where had I seen so much of this? The Trinity? The Little Deschutes? It had slipped in the telescoping of rivers.

I couldn't float the entire slot without lining part of it. So I covered the bottom of my first casts, doping out the drift as I did, and preparing for the long float in the heart of the spot, one I was sure would raise a fish. The slot was on the left-hand side of the river and contoured the bank, but the riffle drained at an angle to it. I saw that a long, straight cast would drag the fly in a hurry. When the first casts to the lower end failed to produce, I tried a reach cast to the right, got a much better drift, then covered the whole slot with a longer throw.

The Henryville Caddis had floated about two yards when a good brown appeared below it like a beam of butter-colored light. It tipped back, and we were tight. The fish held in the current even though my rod was bent into the cork, then shot out into the shallows for a wild aerial fight. I got it close three times but it managed to churn off through the shallow water. Finally, I had it and turned its cold form upside down in my hand, checked its length against my rod—eighteen inches—and removed the hook. I decided that these were the yellowest, prettiest stream-bred browns I had ever seen. I turned it over and lowered it into the current. I love the feeling when they realize they are free. There seems to be an amazed pause. Then they shoot out of your hand as though you could easily change your mind.

The afternoon wore on without specific event. The middle of a bright day can be as dull as it is timeless. Visibility is so perfect you forget it is seldom a confidence builder for trout. The little imperfections of the leader, the adamant crinkles standing up from the surface, are clear to both parties.

No sale.

But the shadows of afternoon seem to give meaning to the angler's day on about the same scale that fall gives meaning to his year. As always, I could feel in the first hints of darkness a mutual alertness between me and the trout. This vague shadow the trout and I cross progresses from equinox to equinox. Our mutuality grows.

A ring opened on the surface. The first rise I had seen. The fish refused my all-purpose Adams, and I moved on. I reached an even-depth, even-speed stretch of slick water that deepened along the right-hand bank for no reason: there was no curve to it. The deep side was in shadow, a great, profound, detail-filled shadow that stood along the thin edge of brightness, the starry surface of moving water in late sun. At the head of this run, a plunge pool made a vertical curtain of bubbles in the right-hand corner. At that point, the turbulence narrowed away to a thread of current that could be seen for maybe twenty yards on the smooth run. Trout were working.

I cast to the lowest fish from my angle below and to the left. The evenness of the current gave me an ideal float free of drag. In a moment of hubris I threw the size 14 Adams, covered the fish nicely for about five minutes while it fed above and below. I worked my way to the head of the pool, covering six other fish. Quickly, I tied on a Royal Wulff, hoping to shock them into submission. Not a single grab. The fish I covered retired until I went on, then resumed feeding. I was losing my light and had been casting in the middle of rising fish for the better part of an hour: head and tail rises with a slight slurp. There were no spinners in the air, and the thread of the current took whatever it was down through the center of the deep water beyond my vision. This was the first time that day the river had asked me to figure something out; and it was becoming clear that I was not going to catch a fish in this run unless I changed my ways.

I was dealing with the selective trout, that uncompromising creature in whose spirit the angler attempts to read his own fortune.

I tucked my shirt deep inside the top of my waders and pulled the drawstring tight. I hooked my last unsuccessful fly in the keeper and reeled the line up. Then I waded into the cold, deep run, below the feeding fish. I felt my weight decreasing against the bottom as I inched toward the thread of current that carried whatever the fish were feeding on. By the time I reached it, I was within inches of taking on the river and barely weighed enough to keep myself from joining the other flotsam in the Missouri headwaters. But—and, as my mother used to say, "it's a big but"—I could see coming toward me, some like tiny sloops, some like minute life rafts unfurling, baetis duns: olive-bodied, clear-winged, and a tidy size 18.

I have such a thing, I thought, in my fly box.

By the time I had moon-walked back to a depth where my weight meant something, I had just enough time to test my failing eyes against the little olive-emergers and a 6X tippet viewed straight over my head in the final light. Finally, the thing was done and I was ready to cast. The fly seemed to float straight downward in the air and down the sucking hole the trout made. It was another short, thick, buttery brown, and it was the one that kept me from flunking my first day on that river. It's hard to know ahead of time which fish is giving the test.

On the Take

Ted Leeson

FOR A FISHERMAN, this idea of the surface inevitably rises to the top, and there's little wonder why this should be so. Fly fishing is a matter of faith, and like all faiths, it contains a central miracle: the rise of a trout to a dry fly.

In his *Physics*, Aristotle explains what he sees as the governing principle of nature—all things seek their origins. Human beings are held to the ground and prevented from flying off into the air because the body is composed of soil and so clings to the earth by virtue of this affinity. By the same logic, the spirit of a man is of heavenly origin and eventually seeks its celestial home. For Aristotle, the soul tends upward; spiritual things naturally rise. This is the only proposition I know of that broaches a metaphysical argument for dry-fly fishing.

The floating fly seems the very thing for which fly fishing was designed. But in fact, intentionally dressing flies for buoyancy and fishing in a manner to keep them afloat are comparatively new innovations. As a deliberate technique, widely practiced, dry-fly fishing is perhaps only a century or so old. Since then, it has transformed the sport. If fly fishing was not invented for the dry fly, it was rein-vented for it, and surface fishing has come to transcend all other approaches in the angling imagination.

That this recent notion has substantially reorganized our thinking about such an old occupation is in itself highly suggestive, particularly since dry-fly fishing, when gauged against the ordinary criteria, generally proves an unremarkable method. Under most circumstances, it is demonstrably not the best way to take fish, especially large ones. It is not the simplest technique—that honor probably goes to the wet fly. Nor is it the most difficult; nymph fishing, done properly, demands more intense concentration, more exacting line control, a keener eye, and quicker reflexes.

Nonetheless, the floating fly draws fishermen with an ineluctable gravity, and the source of this attraction is not difficult to locate. It originates in a flash, in the abrupt and certain take of a trout. Few moments in fishing hold the same immediacy and vividness as the rise to a floating fly, and none are endowed with the same satisfying sense of closure. In an instant, the take creates dry-fly fishing, separating it from all other techniques, and defining its most compelling attraction.

Dry-fly fishing emerges on the far side of "what happens" and fixes itself on the idea of "where," on the focal plane of the surface. Here, the symmetrical domains of air and water converge to form both a mirror and a barrier. And I think that the fascination of the dry fly arises from this paradoxical character of the surface, at once hinting richly at the life below, while obscuring our apprehension of it.

This capacity to reveal and conceal simultaneously is most apparent in the visual sense. The swells, slicks, roils, and riffles answer to the workings of deeper currents and streambed topographies, tracing, if imperfectly, the hidden contours of the river. Yet at the same time the fluctuating and reflective surface inhibits our ability to see beneath it.

The particular nature of this restriction is significant, for we are overwhelmingly visual creatures—in both the way we describe and operate in our world, and, more importantly, the way we know it. Our discourse abounds in words and expressions that equate vision with understanding: "I see" denotes recognition and comprehension; to "shed some light on the subject" metaphorically unites the perception of the eye with that of the mind; to put something "in perspective" suggests an intellectual ordering that derives from visual, spatial relationships. "To be enlightened," "to bring something out in the open," "to make it clear" (or "to remain in the dark")— in a hundred such usages we equate our capacity to know with our capacity to see. And the same equation lies at the heart of angling's most telling phrase, "reading the water," which links a visual process with an analytical one.

Riding on the surface, a dry fly becomes a point of contact between the world of the fisherman and that of the fish, the nexus of eye and mind. It is the visual extension of our imagination, probing what can't be seen and charting the shape of human inquisitiveness and expectancy. A drifting fly is a test, a series of questions inscribed on the surface: "Are the trout here?" "Have I alarmed them?" "Does the fly pattern adequately resemble something that belongs in this place?"—in short, "Have I accurately inferred and observed the principles by which the river works?"

At the instant of the take, the boundary of the surface is shattered. Hidden things are disclosed. We have tempted a separate world to reveal itself to us, to our eyes and imaginations. The take is the visual analog of an answered question, a curiosity satisfied, the visible confirmation that we have, if only locally and temporarily, understood some small thing about a river: the dynamics of its atmosphere; the habits of its trout; their mechanisms of predation; the character of their instincts. The take transports us, imaginatively, from one domain to another. And although human characteristics are commonly ascribed to fish behavior— "curiosity," "playfulness," "rage"—in fact, quite the opposite is true. When a fish takes a fly, it hasn't become more manlike; rather, the angler has become more fishlike. Each cast tries the limits of the river; each take successfully integrates us into its processes and offers an increment of understanding.

Much of fishing is a physical experience, an electric and buoyant thrill like bubbles in the blood. But the take is a subtler affair that appeals to the intellect and awareness. For even the surface itself, the boundary we fish on, is itself an imaginative construct. In reality, only the water and air exist; the interface between them—some third, separate place we call the "surface"—is something we create. Our brains are not wired to accept the deep anarchy of absolute disjunction, and so we invent thresholds and zones of transition that soothe our understanding with little continuities and make us feel better. The surface of the river is a hypothetical fulcrum, balancing the aquatic world with our own imperfect grasp of it. On this plane of our own invention, we cast our surmise, wonder, and hope bound up in so much feather and fur.

The take instantaneously validates our efforts, conferring a measure of definitiveness and closure to an enterprise otherwise riddled with uncertainty and inconclusiveness. Few things in life, I think, have this to offer. A rising trout is an upward-tending thing, and the surface of a river is the ceiling of its world with all the clarifying power of altitude.

At the Second Bend Pool

Nick Lyons

THE EAST BRANCH, skirting the base of the bench, thick with willows, cattails, and marsh, bore little resemblance to the West Branch or the main stem of Spring Creek. It was a moody, mysterious place. The water was thinner here, and there were fewer bends. In only a run or two, and usually only within inches of the far bank, could you expect to raise a fish on a fly that did not actually imitate a living insect. The fishing was more exacting and the entire attitude of the river here was different, and had a different effect on me.

Herb had not taken me to it for the first ten days, and of course there had been no reason to do so, for we had more than enough fishing elsewhere, especially when the Green Drakes were on. And there was less water here, barely enough for two people to fish comfortably. There was the huge pondlike pool in which we had both taken those large fish, the slick thin head where water from the river flattened and spread; three pools; and then a second huge pondlike pool. Above the second pond, the river grew even more mysterious and wild—and was extremely difficult to fish. I kept saving these East Branch headwaters for a more leisurely day. I kept thinking that some day I'd spend six or seven hours up there, track it to its source, wander a bit and perhaps fish a bit, and see what I could find. Meanwhile, whenever I went up the East Branch, I thought about those headwaters, even as the lower East Branch itself made me strangely contemplative.

One day I caught a marvelous hatch of PMDs where the river went into the first pond, then caddis and PMDs in the First Bend Pool, and more rising fish in the middle run. By 11:00 A.M., I'd taken nearly a dozen good trout, all big browns and one twenty-inch rainbow, and had had more than my fill. I'd fished very hard the day before and this burst of action—and success—had bled me of much of my usual ambition. So I decided to sit down on that pleasant inside rim of the Second Bend Pool and merely watch the water.

That great cluster of fish were in the deep hole—thirty or forty of them, in all age classes, and a couple of fish were rising steadily. But I put my rod down in the high grasses and got out a little black notebook I always carry in a vest pocket. Usually I'm too busy to write in it; usually when I'm on the water I want only to fish. But I had been fishing hard, every day for more than three weeks, and I had caught a lot of fish, and I rather wanted to write about those fish I'd found rising in the slick at the head of the pond. I'd had to cast across and slightly downstream to get them and that hour had been exceptionally pleasant. It was best to fish not as I usually did, when I could, but when the fishing would be best—and slowly I had been learning, because of the enormous number of opportunities at Spring Creek, when that best was. The morning had been a revelation; I had not known that the bigger fish, from the pond, would move up during a good PMD hatch, though it was logical that a good head of flies would bring them there. I noted that the first of them had risen at about 10:45, and promised myself I'd come back the next day to see if it was a daily event. I had seen fish move steadily upstream during a hatch, ever closer to the source of a hatch, several times; and I had also seen them, in the big flat, slip back downstream during a heavy hatch, taking flies lower and lower in the pool, using less and less energy and drifting back with the current. I never went to Spring Creek without seeing something new; it was so fecund, so full of chances, that I don't think even Herb had seen all of it, nor would anyone, ever.

A snout came up in the current of the Second Bend Pool but I decided not to pursue it.

I was scribbling rather quickly now.

Learning something new about angling always excites my brain—what would take a specific fish, why it was feeding, how to solve an individual angling problem. I'd done something right and I wanted to understand what. The general laws of angling never held for all situations but they always overlapped. You learned the parts of speech, one at a time, and then you tried to put them all together: not parts anymore, but speech.

There was a "speech" to the writing about fishing, too, and I'd thought hard about its many different languages. Literary friends told me that the great trick was not to use the technical language of fly fishing—the thorax spinners, the 7X leader tippets, the *Hexagenias* and Tricos and PMDs. These, they said, were the jargon of the sport and made it quite unavailable to the intelligent general reader, he who did not fish but read with care and discernment. I'm sure this is so. But the technical language is not the voice of the idiot savant except when it is used by an idiot savant. And I wasn't after a language of literature.

Just as I would not write down, I would not write up. What I was doing, I hoped, with as much skill and invisible artifice as I could muster—as little of the factitious, the posturing as possible—was to report on days afield, and the nature of my relationship to the sport, a relationship that included having, at various times, the keenest possible interest in the minutiae of fly fishing: not using the fancy or occult words, or the Latin, or the names of people and places to impress, but choosing, always, the fullest, most personal way to tell where I'd been. A Trico is a Trico is a Trico; it is not merely a small black fly, nor is it a rose.

I had tried, for more than twenty-five years, to find and to build a language that represented me—something with feeling but not sentimentality, a voice playful but not mannered, not down, not up, not safe, not different just to be different. Some clever populist once wrote to a fishing magazine complaining of the literary references in essays I wrote—to Yeats, Keats, Kafka, and Chaucer—as if these had been laid on with a trowel, with pretensions. He had deliberately misspelled every other word in his letter, feigning a superior ignorance, to defend something called the common man. But I read Yeats and Keats and Kafka in my twenties, on my own, and they changed my life. I wouldn't think of hiding them. They are as much my friends as Len and Mike and Doug; they are as much a part of my speech as Tricos and 7X tippets. Do we read books to get bland pap or mere information or clever nonsense, or to touch another human being? I want those who read me to touch me, to know me—for better or worse—not some studied mask I might put on. And this is the stew of me: Yeats and PMDs, wit that leavens and builds proportion, not sophisticated but (I hope) not dumb, a warm mulch that heats the postmodernist chill. I'd like the stew to be rich enough to catch some of the stillness, complexity, joy, fierce intensity, frustration, practicality, hilarity, fascination, satisfaction that I find in fly fishing. I'd like it to be fun, because fly fishing is fun— not ever so serious and self-conscious that I take it to be either a religion or a way of life, or a source of salvation. I like it passionately but I try to remember what Cézanne once said after a happy day of fishing: he'd had lots of fun, but it "doesn't lead far."

I'd like fish talk to exist not by itself, as a separate estate, but in relationship to scores of other languages that live in me, from art language to street talk to the voices of a thousand writers who echo in my head: not them, nor the echo of them, but something absolutely mine, as real a possession as a Sony Trinitron or a Winston rod or my grandfather's oak dining table.

Perhaps, I thought, sitting on the inside rim of the Second Bend Pool, I am not after trout at all; perhaps this is a ruse; perhaps, among my many ulterior motives, one is the discovery of a language. Or has writing about fishing, which cannot occur without first fishing, become quite as important to me as the act itself? "Wouldn't think of disassociating Fishing from Art," said the happy John Marin—"one and the same thing with me."

A trout shoves its snout up, my heart beats quicker, and I doubt all ulterior motives.

I would as well be here, beside this pool, right now, as anywhere in the universe. I have thought about such a place without knowing it existed. At times I have wished life as simple as this riverbank—the world a logical structure of bend, current, riffle, and pool, the drama already unfolding on the glassy surface, and me, here on the bank, my ass wet, armed with some simple lovely balanced tools and some knowledge, prepared to become part of it for a few moments.

A fish rises with a slight spreading circle; then another comes up, its snout rising from its world up into mine, of air; the drama begins. In a while I may choose to enter it, or I may not, for I have learned enough skills to play; I can cast beyond my shoelaces.

This is a contained, mostly understandable world, and in my nearly sixty years I have understood less rather than more of that other, outside world. Like Kafka, I sometimes seem to hop about bewildered among my fellow men—and they often regard me with deep suspicion. That larger world, away from rivers—and my little place in it—stuns me with its complexity: The old friend who last month looked me in the eye and lied. The other who stole from me. Incrementing details and details. People with Rolodexes for brains. "The beating down of the wise/And great Art beaten down and down." That bewildering bear I have been—rife with contradictions. The demons in me that demand more of friends than they can ever give, and nothing; that want only solitude like this—and the rush and lights and edge of the cities; that like and crave and despise all "getting and spending."

Tolstoy speaks of an uncle who once told him, when he was a boy, to go into a corner and *not* think about a white bear. I have come to this riverbank, this rarest of corners of the universe, and of course cannot help but think of all that other jazz, and perhaps always will. Pascal says that the trouble with the western world is that we don't know how to be content in an empty room. I am not content here—or anywhere. Nor, as I think of it at the Second Bend Pool, do I want to be content, like a cow or a holy man. I want to put boulders in the way; I don't want to flow without effort. I am restless—therefore I am. And here, now, it's best to get most of it out—like a good sneeze, god-blessed or not.

A muskrat surfaces in the slack shank of the bend, sees me just as I turn and see him—"Since things in motion sooner catch the eye/Than what not stirs"—and, in a lithe gray roll, porpoises and disappears. I follow his wake across the river, into the marsh, up out of the water and into a hole on the opposite bank; he never looks back.

There are more circles and snouts now. I may have been here half an hour or an hour or two hours and the world here feels quite safe from my possible predation. On the glassy surface, a couple of feet from my eyes, I see some flattened spent spinners, two mottled caddis, and half a dozen lovely Pale Morning Duns. I pick out one of the duns with my eye, one golden speck twenty-five feet out; it reflects the midday sun as it carries on the current and disappears in a rather full and satisfied pocking of the water. The trout here take the duns like that when they get going good. It's unnerving to see them do so. They are as vulnerable now as they'll ever be.

I tie on a parachute PMD, daub it with flotant, strip line off my reel, and make a first tentative cast. But my heart is not in it and the cast is too tentative. I have been thinking too much. The line lands heavily, well short of the nearest rise, and suddenly the pool is perfectly still, as if it contained not a minnow.

Well, I have been snubbed before, by trout and Diana Vreeland, and am sure these fish will come back. Anyway, my brain hasn't quite stopped nibbling on my concentration. And there is no place I'd rather be right now—not Paris, where the fishing is poor; not the beach, where you are asked to take off your clothes in public, put grease on your body, sit in the sand; not the great libraries or concert halls or even the museums I love. This valley feels like home to me right now— me, a city kid, descended from Russian city people, bent always, in a kind of hungry tropism, to space and clear water and open sky.

I would like to be here for weeks, even months, but I could not live all my life in trout country. I have other fish to fry and, difficult as that other world might be, I'd rather be in the thick of it, blasted by its terrors, than sit outside and snipe. If all the year were holidays, to sport would be as tedious as to work—and I have rarely found work tedious. And in the city I can stand before a Rembrandt self-portrait, a Velázquez, a Titian, a delicate Tiepolo, and be in some vital connection with the real thing: not some predigested version of it in a magazine, a reproduction in a book, part of a short course on television, but the real thing. Someone out this way, some years ago, called my Picasso a fraud and wondered how I could teach "Keats, Shelley, and all those weirdos." In my office, things other than trout rise, and some of them "lead far."

Why must I always compare them?

Why, when both are so important to me, must I hold one against the other?

Is it that they always bleed into each other and are never wholly separate?

Or that, looking always for one simple and direct view of this stew of a world, I am tugged in just a few too many directions?

The fish have started to feed again. There are two in the main current, slurping; one dimples in the slack water near the far bank; several are high enough in the water for their dorsals to poke through the slate surface.

I might have been trying for two hours to do something vaguely called "getting in touch with yourself and with nature," but now, with the fish rising freely, I have something specific to do and all that is irrelevant. If I have "gotten in touch" with anything it's the damp bank against which I've been leaning, the grasses soggy from spring seepage; mostly my elbow and ass, sopping wet, have been in touch.

I watch a teal with a string of five or six ducklings, like a tail, slip up out of the pool and around the bend. I see a couple of killdeer chicks, the size of golf balls, scurry into the underbrush.

The fish are going good now.

I check my fly, draw enough line from my reel, look at the simple happy scene before me, of five or six rising trout—and then calmly tattoo them.

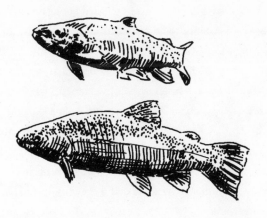

Sudden Spate: A New Generation of Fresh, Literate Books About Trout Fishing

Robert H. Berls

THE EDITOR OF *TROUT* MAGAZINE asked me to choose the best fishing books of the last thirty years. He set two constraints: The books selected had to be about fishing for salmonids, of course, and not have been published before 1959 when Trout Unlimited was founded. There could be no post-1959 reprints, second editions or books first published in France in 1957 (as when I mentioned I was considering Charles Ritz's *A Fly Fisher's Life*). Oh yes, there was one other rule: He said he would pound my eyeballs out if I didn't include Robert Traver's *Trout Madness,* presumably because he admires it so—or maybe because he hopes to be invited to fish Frenchman's Pond.

The deal was that I would select the best books, say why they were so, and out-line the changes in fishing books over the last thirty years. In turn I got to set some ground rules. To simplify the task, I excluded books on casting and fly tying, primers, and books on Atlantic salmon or steelhead. This last needs an explana-tion. I know nothing about steelhead, except what I read, and little about salmon, so I am not willing to pass judgment in print on books whose content is *aqua incognita* to me. But if I did, I believe one of Roderick Haig-Brown's books that have appeared since 1959, either *Fisherman's Fall* (1964) or *Fisherman's Summer* (1959), would be here. The late Harmon Henkin, a good writer "in his own write," as John Lennon would have said, called Haig-Brown, in a *New York Times* article a few years ago, "the finest all-around angling writer this continent has yet produced." (Never mind that he was born and grew up in England.) So peace to the pursuers of anadromy.

I need to tell you that some of my favorite angling authors are not here—and why. Either they have not written books, or not books about trout fishing, or they are best known for their magazine articles: Bill Barich, Harrison O'Connor, David Quammen, Charles Waterman.

There are other favorites whose books are not here owing to boundary disputes: William Humphrey, Tom McGuane, Red Smith. Humphrey's *Open Season* (1986) is an admirable book, but it's more about hunting, saltwater, or salmon than it is about trout. The chapter on fishing for Walleye and Carp in the Seine in the cen-ter of Paris is worth the price of the book. Tom McGuane's *An Outside Chance, Essays on Sport* (1980) has some fine trout-fishing writing in it surrounded by other kinds of outdoor adventures. (I have read only one of McGuane's half-dozen nov-els and didn't like it much. But that's unfair to the author: it's akin to reading only one of Shakespeare's plays, a lesser one, and concluding that his reputation is exag-gerated.) McGuane did the film script for *Rancho Deluxe*—the only movie you're likely to see that opens in Dan Bailey's flyshop—a movie I enjoyed immensely.

Red Smith's (the late *New York Times* and Pulitzer Prize-winning sports writer) columns on fishing were collected in the prosaically titled *Red Smith on Fishing* (1963), a little book that deserves reprinting, preferably augmented with more of Red's trout-fishing columns, especially those on Sparse Grey Hackle. Smith is best known for his writing on spectator sports, especially baseball, the fights, and horseracing, but as his biographer Ira Berkow said in *Red* (1986): "Besides the English language and social drinking, Smith's greatest hobby was fishing, prefer-ably trout-fishing." But Smith's little book has as much saltwater, salmon, and bass in it as trout. It would be hard not to like a book with the following sort of anecdote in it. Smith occasionally returned to his native Wisconsin to fish the lakes for smallmouth bass. On one of these trips with his small son, they retired from the lakes in the hot middays to crossroads taverns to cool themselves each to his own need. The boy, wolfing down a sandwich and a Coke, observed: "'Gee, Dad, this is the life, ain't it? Fishing and eating in saloons.'"

The thirty years since 1959 have seen an acceleration of a trend toward imitation in fly fishing that began, if we need a landmark, in 1935 with Preston Jennings's *A Book of Trout Flies*. What Jennings began was continued in the 1940s and 1950s with James Leisenring's *The Art of Tying the Wet Fly* (1941), Charles Wetzel's *Practical Fly Fishing* (1943) and *Trout Flies, Naturals and Imitations* (1955), Art Flick's *Streamside Guide to Naturals and Their Imitations* (1947), Vincent Marinaro's *A Modern Dry Fly Code* (1950), and Ernest Schwiebert's *Matching the Hatch* in 1955.

The trickle of books on imitative fly fishing that appeared over those twenty years, and which can be held literally in one hand, did not constitute the center of fly fishing in the United States. Paul Schullery, in his *American Fly Fishing*, noted that Jennings's book was out of the mainstream and ran counter to the prevailing attitude that imitation of the natural insect was unnecessary. Anglers, especially dry fly anglers, concentrated on presenting a drag-free fly to the trout and paid less attention to fly choice.

123

Leisenring's book and Wetzel's first book almost vanished without trace and Marinaro's book was remaindered. But the imitation school has taken what Schullery called the "moral high ground in fly-fishing writing." The American presentation school of dry fly fishing exemplified by George LaBranche and Ray Bergman has gradually been supplanted as the mainstream of writing about trout fly fishing by the imitationist approach. The presentation school still has advocates, however, most recently, Art Lee in his book *Fishing Dry Flies for Trout on Rivers and Streams* (1982).

The danger in clinging to one approach to trout fishing is reductionism: the belief that fly fishing for trout can be reduced to one simple explanation when the matter is varied and complex. H.L. Mencken, the sage of Baltimore, observed that for any complex question "there is almost always a simple answer—that is almost always wrong." In a brilliant essay on historical forces, *The Hedgehog and the Fox*, Sir Isaiah Belrin analyzed statesmen and political theorists as foxes who know many things or as hedgehogs who know one big thing. Rewarding fly fishing for trout cannot be reduced to one single answer. We should not dive down a hole grasping one big truth. Presentation versus imitation is a false dichotomy: Both are needed and more.

Gradually, the presentationist approach is being absorbed into the imitation school and transformed into a holistic approach to fly fishing. Fred Arbona, in his excellent book *Mayflies, the Angler, and the Trout* (1980), addressed the north–south magnetic pulls of the presentationist and imitative schools, and advised the angler to "adopt the most rational and advantageous approach—that which incorporates the best of these two worlds." Charles Brooks advocated fishing the right fly, in the right place, in the right way. Datus Proper treats presentation as part of imitation.

Before anointing the chosen few you need to know what selection criteria were used. W.H. Auden observed that "goodness is easier to recognize than to define." But I rush in to attempt definitions.

The film industry refers to movies with staying power as having "legs." So I was seeking books with legs. Books that last possess originality: they have something important and new to say. Too many trout fishing books remind me of Gotthold Lessing's (the eighteenth-century German Enlightenment writer and scholar) one-sentence book review: "What is true isn't new and what is new isn't true." Books selected need to be well-researched and provide insight—from the research or from distilled experience. They need to be well-written. For works of entertainment, being well-written is essential. For books of instruction the writing must be clear, so that the medium doesn't fog up the message. A master of English prose, George Orwell, told us how in his famous essay on "Politics and the English Language." Good prose is like a windowpane, "clear and transparent." Too many angling writers, as William Humphrey said, try to write beautifully before being able to write well. Angling books also ought to acknowledge their sources; many do not, thereby presenting another's work as their own. And they have to pass the laugh test of credibility as to the numbers and sizes of fish caught. British books, for this contest, had to have influence in this country. Many good British angling books do not—to our loss.

The books on method selected here have reshaped my thinking about fly fishing for trout, making me think about the sport in new and different ways. The books of record (and there is often overlap between these and books of instruction) are books I want to consult again and again. The books of entertainment must provide delight for that is their reason for being. The best combine instruction and entertainment as in, for example, Haig-Brown's works. All must jump-start the imagination.

Favorite Fifteen: Books of Record and Instruction

Leonard Wright noted in his fascinating *Fly-Fishing Heresies* (1975) that in the United States we had no single reference work of angling entomology to put beside Alfred Ronalds's *The Fly-Fisher's Entomology* published a century before Preston Jennings's book. Ronalds's work, the first to correlate the technical and common names, is more comprehensive than Jennings's, but it is easier to be comprehensive in Britain where there are only fifty or so species of mayflies compared to our ten times that many. Jennings confined his researches to New York, New Jersey, and Pennsylvania, and only parts of them; Wetzel restricted himself to Pennsylvania; Flick kept to the Catskills and largely to one stream, the Schoharie. Schwiebert's *Matching the Hatch* was the first to attempt to cover the entire country, but Schwiebert admitted that his book was not a complete guide to even the important hatches and stated that it would be many years before our leading hatches are classified.

Selective Trout, Doug Swisher and Carl Richards (1971), and *Hatches,* Al Caucci and Bob Nastasi (1975).

125

These two books were a major advance in charting the aquatic insects and important hatches of our trout streams—especially the mayflies. Both go well beyond anything previously available and in a form intended for anglers. Both incorporate extensive research on aquatic insects on the stream and with aquariums, and their identification, biology, hatching behavior and imitation. All this is arduous and time consuming, and few anglers have the ambition and commitment to see it through.

Hatches and *Selective Trout* are major works of record and instruction that deserve study by serious anglers. Not many anglers will read them through more than once but they deserve frequent consultation—dipping into them and re-reading as need or whim indicates. An innovation of both books was the large color photos of adult and immature insects: Jennings, Schwiebert and Wetzel had none, and Flick had only small ones.

Swisher's and Richards's frustrations with trout feeding selectively to hatches drove them to research on what was hatching, where and when, but also, because of dissatisfaction with standard fly patterns, to try to find better imitations. Their contributions to more effective flies re-introduced the no-hackle dry fly (which has had a major influence), revived the parachute dun, increased attention to spinners and emergers and brought fresh thinking to the problems of imitation. Caucci and Nastasi introduced the Comparadun, a hairwing no-hackle now in common use, along with Swisher's and Richards's quill wing no-hackle, on spring creeks and other often difficult flat-water streams. *Hatches* is better on the natural insects; *Selective Trout* is better on fly imitation.

Both *Hatches* and *Selective Trout* were important contributions, and had palpable impact on anglers, but the work is nowhere near done. Datus Proper said that "at present no single work gives us all we need to know, even about mayflies in the eastern United States, let alone about all kinds of flies in all regions." Proper believes that angling entomologies will have to become "deep and narrow, covering single biological zones; perhaps even single major rivers." Leonard Wright points to a similar stream not 40 miles from Flick's Schoharie "where half of the important insects bear no resemblance to Flick's . . ."

In *A Modern Dry Fly Code*, Vincent Marinaro said that the writers "of ancient fame" such as Halford and Ronalds defined imitation by "human vision and comprehension, supported only by the prop of entomology." That way alone lies grave error, Marinaro continued, "since it does not take into account the vision of the trout and the geometry of the underwater world . . ." Marinaro believed that trout vision and the physics of refraction of light in water "are the dominant factors in devising imitations."

126

In his *Code* (my vote for the best American fly-fishing book), Marinaro asserted that the angler must, "recognize the (trout's) rise form which identifies the taking of any particular species if he is to select the proper artificial." Here, Marinaro agreed with G.E.M. Skues who believed that "the due appreciation of *how* a trout is rising forms the very essence of fishing, whether it be with floating fly or artificial nymph—and it is often no easy matter."

In *The Ring of the Rise*, Vincent C. Marinaro (1976). In his second book Marinaro concentrated his great skills on adding two more props to successful imitation: what the trout sees and the anatomy of the trout's rise. In the most remarkable photographs of rising trout ever taken, Marinaro dissected several rise forms: the simple rise, compound, complex, the long drift, the sipping rise, and the swivel. Careful study of this series will help the angler to achieve what Marinaro calls "the ultimate sophistication in fly fishing . . . the ability to read and interpret the different kinds of rise forms." Marinaro acknowledged that "it is an uncommon skill." His photos are a major learning aid for the serious angler, since the disaggregation of the rise form is difficult for the unaided human eye.

In photos taken with the aid of a slant tank, Marinaro analyzed the physics of light refraction in water to fix how and where a trout sees a fly, and how flies should be designed to make use of that knowledge. Then in "Fishing to the Ring of the Rise," Marinaro discussed fly presentation in light of how the trout sees and rises.

The rest of his book is a collection of previously published articles, but they are plummy with wisdom and as imaginative as anything Marinaro ever wrote— particularly "A Game of Nods" and "The Hidden Hatch."

Marinaro "crossed over the last iron bridge," as Datus Proper put it, in 1986.

Datus C. Proper took imitation by "human vision and comprehension" and turned it upside down. In *What the Trout Said About the Design of Trout Flies and Other Mysteries* (1982), Proper's enormous contribution was to shift focus from flies that look like imitations to us to what look like imitations to the trout. What looks right to them may not look right to us. The traditional approach derived from Halford is to call flies imitative only when they appeared so to human eyes. This tradition was passed down to us via Theodore Gordon and Jennings. Proper puts that tradition on its head and makes us think about flies from the trout's point of view—thus the book's title. *127*

Secondly, Proper compels us to stop thinking about flies as patterns, which are primarily color variations, and forces us to think about fly *design*: why and how flies should be constructed to affect their behavior first (which includes presentation) as well as size, shape, and color. The rise of a trout to an artificial is triggered by the design of the fly more than by pattern, by how a fly behaves more than its color. That is what the trout say.

Fly patterns number in the hundreds or thousands representing, as Marinaro said, "the accumulated debris of five centuries of fly-tying disorder. Much of this is complicated by patterns that do not express any theory of imitation . . ." The third great virtue of *What the Trout Said* is that it distills Proper's vast experience observing how trout react to different fly designs under demanding conditions into a theory of imitation. (The psychologist Kurt Lewin asserted that there is nothing so practical as a good theory.)

Proper writes entertainingly, even delightfully, uncommon in books of instruction: only Marinaro (and Haig-Brown) can play in his league.

When I began to select books for this article I was inclined, for reasons of simplification, to admit only American authors to the winners' circle. But *The Trout and the Fly, A New Approach* by John Goddard and Brian Clarke (1980) forced its way in through the strength of its qualities by influencing serious trout anglers in this country.

As with Marinaro's *Ring*, Goddard and Clarke conducted extensive underwater experiments and observations on how trout see the fly and the angler. They learned that, complementary to Marinaro's observations and Proper's conclusions, light and its refraction make the fly look very different to the trout below from the way it does to the angler above. Their instream observations with cameras in the stream bottom, and with observation tanks, revealed which characteristics of the fly, transformed by the physics of light as it moves through the trout's mirror and window, trigger the trout to rise. This is supported by color photos of trout feeding behavior, the geometric world underwater, and the trigger to the rise. Their instream and observation tank photography of what the trout sees of the fly goes beyond anything done yet. Goddard and Clarke, supported by revealing photos, show us how to see the trout, where they lie, and clues to how they feed. They also provide novel techniques for fishing the dry fly and the nymph and reading the take to the nymph.

The Trout and the Fly is of the greatest importance to those who fish for difficult, experienced trout in flat waters, but it is of immense value to any fly fisherman. Once you have read and pondered the implications of their experiments and observations on, like Proper's book, the interaction of fly "design" and the effects on trout you will not think about trout and flies and imitation in the same way again. A reader cannot ask for much more from a book.

The writers on fly fishing for trout have neglected the caddisfly, possibly because the native language of fly fishing is mostly English. The classic study (it became a model for later research) on the feeding habits of trout was done in 1936 on the River Don in Scotland. The Don is accepted as the best trout river in Scotland, probably because of its fertile limestone valley. But caddisflies accounted for only five percent of the insect fauna in the Don. This may explain, as Gary LaFontaine said, the emphasis on mayflies in the British fly fishing literature. It would be hard to find, LaFontaine said, a North American trout stream where the insect fauna is only five percent caddisflies.

Caddisflies (1981) by Gary LaFontaine is a model of what an angling entomology should be: ten years of research in the scientific literature (150 or so papers and books are in his bibliography plus many more in the footnotes), instream research, including more than three years of scuba diving observation and experiment, research using aquariums and fluvariums, extensive identification work, plus lots of help from other angler-entomologists, and the results subjected to the scrutiny of professional entomologists.

Caddisflies is in two parts: part two, the biology of caddisflies, which goes far beyond that of other angling entomologies, delves deeply into caddisfly habitat, biology, caddis as a food source for trout, and insect emergence and egg-laying charts. Part one is devoted to tying and fishing caddisfly imitations.

LaFontaine does not just support his theory of caddisfly imitation with what Marinaro called "the prop of entomology" for he bases it on his research into the underwater perceptions of the trout—which makes for some of the most fascinating reading in an absorbing book. LaFontaine used his underwater observations to identify which aspects of the insect's behavior and physical characteristics triggered the trout to prey upon it—often in preference to other prey at the time. These triggering characteristics were then designed into his flies. The finished flies were then observed underwater against competing flies. Some of these imitations have become established designs in caddis pupae imitations.

In *The Trout and the Fly,* Goddard and Clarke asserted that presentation versus imitation is a sterile dispute, that "for consistent results with experienced fish, one must be able to deliver the correct fly in the correct way." Charles Brooks would only add "and in the right place."

In *The Trout and the Stream* (1974), Charles Brooks wants to move anglers beyond the common approach of smothering the stream with a fly in chuck-and-chance-it style. Although "shockingly inefficient," it is the most popular method, Brooks believes, because "it requires no thinking."

Brooks's approach, what he wants to teach, is to know where trout live and feed, what they feed on in different types of water, and how to fish a representative fly in such a way that the trout will believe it is real. His credo is that "one can definitely increase his pleasure by increasing his knowledge." When he catches a fish he wants to know why and, when he does not, he wants to know why not.

What Brooks does better than anyone else is to analyze and describe water types, trout lies, and insect populations and behavior in those various water types.

This is the first part of his book: life in running water, the requirements of trout, and knowing rivers. After teaching you the fundamentals, Brooks takes you by the hand, shows you how to fish the water and what to fish it with. These two parts are the heart of his book, one that bears frequent re-reading. Writing in a vigorous if homespun style, Brooks was the first and still the best angling writer to begin to systematize Rocky Mountain fly fishing. His recent death is a grievous loss.

Parallel to the trend toward imitation is another major trend in fly fishing, the nymph. If G.E.M. Skues didn't exactly invent the nymph, he put it on the map in 1910 with his landmark book *Minor Tactics of the Chalk Stream*. (Skues gets my vote as the most important fly fishing author of the twentieth century.) His major accomplishment among many was recovering the old wet fly art and transforming it for modern conditions on the chalk stream.

The hares Skues started are still running strongly.

One of the modern exponents of the nymph is Gary A. Borger. His *Nymphing, a Basic Book* (1979) is a model of what a how-to book should be. There is more information, even wisdom, packed into this little book than in most method books several times larger.

Although he begins with the basics, Borger quickly moves into more advanced techniques, and any angler who masters them will have put himself through a doctoral level course in the modern wet fly. Borger doesn't rely on glossy photos of big trout or scenes in exotic locations to impress the reader. He gives you the straight stuff and so much of it that if one reads it, fishes the nymph seriously for a few years and reads it again and again, one begins to appreciate it and to make full use of it. I have read his book several times, studied it, and read it again for this article; I'm still learning from it and expect to keep on so. If a beginner or an experienced dry fly man—not yet a nymph fisherman—asked me what book on nymphing to go to I would unhesitatingly recommend Borger's. Charles Brooks's *Nymph Fishing for Larger Trout* (1976) is a close-run second choice.

Borger writes clear, vigorous prose and makes every word count—unlike that nineteenth-century British sporting writer Nimrod, who, as Bill Barich pointed out in his *Traveling Light* (1984), never used two words when six would do.

Early in his *American Fly Fishing, a History* (1987), Paul Schullery observed that not much yet is known about the beginnings of fly fishing in Europe. But thanks to his assiduousness we know much about the origins and history of fly fishing in

North America. Schullery has written the most comprehensive history of the beginnings and evolution of fly fishing here, even though he admits that "we have a lot to learn about early American fly fishing."

Much past writing about the history of fly fishing has actually been bibliographic essays, a literature review of angling authors and their books. John Waller Hills's *A History of Fly Fishing for Trout* (1921), on the British tradition and a book I admire, is a review of the prominent literature. The same is true of the chapters on the evolution of fly fishing in Ernest Schwiebert's colossal failure, *Trout*. To write history requires not only reading landmark books, but also excavation in dusty archives, reading published and unpublished correspondence, scouting out diaries and manuscripts, and tracking down the fugitive literature in obscure periodicals. Writing history only from landmark books can be done, but at a price. Ernest Hemingway believed that a writer can only omit what he knows about, or else he omits at his risk and may leave soft places in his writing. Schullery said that we still want a good literary history of American writing on fly fishing—he admits he could only cover it peripherally.

Schullery has blazed the frontiers of American fly fishing. Others will need to fill in details and extend the boundaries if they can.

131

Favorite Fifteen: Books of Entertainment

William Zinsser, in his excellent guide, *On Writing Well,* said, "The writing that we most admire over the years—the King James Bible, Abraham Lincoln, E.B. White, Red Smith—is writing that has the strength of simplicity."

Whenever Red Smith was stuck for a column, he knew that a telephone call to Sparse Grey Hackle would deliver one on a platter. Sparse seemed to know everyone and everything in the world of trout fishing and was generous with his knowledge. Red Smith, not long before his own death, gave a eulogy for another writer and said: "Dying is no big deal. Living is the trick." In a long life Sparse did a lot of living, from serving with the New York Militia Field Artillery on the Mexican Border Patrol to driving an ambulance in France in World War One; and a lot of fishing especially on his beloved Beaverkill and Neversink. Arnold Gingrich anointed him dean of American fly fishermen, describing him as the last link in a tradition back through Sparse's friends Hewitt and LaBranche to the Theodore Gordon era.

Some of the best of Sparse's living and fishing are recorded in prose that has the "strength of simplicity" in his *Fishless Days, Angling Nights* (1971). There are a lot of reasons to read Sparse's book, but the best are his stories and memories that come, like an old race horse saving his best for the stretch, at the end of the book evoking the golden age of Catskill fly fishing with the Brooklyn Fly Fishers Club on the Beaverkill and Edward R. Hewitt's "five princely miles" of water on the Neversink. These pieces along with fishing on the Brodhead with Richard C. Hunt, another prominent angler of the golden age, and Roy Steenrod's and Herman Christian's memories of the old days in the Catskills when "you could fish the river for a month without seeing a man . . . " are worth whatever you have to pay to buy a copy these days. In addition, as a lagniappe, you get such charm-ing pieces as "Who Is Sparse Grey Hackle?" and "A Drink of Water." Sparse died in 1983 at the age of 91. There is no replacement.

In his history of the Peloponnesian War, Thucydides says that stories happen only to people who can tell them. Stories keep happening to Robert Traver. Like Scheherazade, Traver may need to tell stories to go on living. No minimalist writer, things happen in his stories. Like all good storytellers, Traver keeps you turning the pages to find out what happens. The stories are, purportedly, true even if they may be embroidered or exaggerated. But then Dr. Johnson told us that "seldom any splendid story is wholly true."

Why is Robert Traver's *Trout Madness* (1960) such an attractive, captivating book? Part of it is the sheer story-telling ability: "Wonders are willingly told and willingly heard," as Dr. Johnson said of the poet Pope. But there is more to the fascination than that irreplaceable attribute. Traver has fished so often, nearly every day for much of his life, and for so long, and kept such records of it all—complete records of every trip back to 1936, he says—that much has happened to him. And when it does happen he keeps close to the bone of his story with vig-orous prose—you always know where you are even if Traver doesn't know where he is, when he is off on another of his frequent, self-described wild goose chases—usually with his crony, the unforgettable A. Luigi (Louie) Bonetti. He isn't what I would call a disciplined writer such as William Humphrey or Tom McGuane and he edges into silliness at times, but I forgive him that. He isn't shy or aloof: He comes at you warts and all and he has the priceless capacity, like Sparse Grey Hackle, of being able to poke fun at his own conceits.

I have not met him, but I feel that I have because of the immense personal charm that radiates from his pages. He strikes me as a man I would want to fish with, drink with, or, if I had to, go into combat with. I am not a lawyer, but if I were I would not want to oppose him in a courtroom.

Bill Parcells, former head coach of the New York Giants, once said that playing professional football is not a game for well-adjusted people. Obsessive fly fishing for trout may not be a game for well-adjusted people either. John Gierach wears clothes just on the respectable side of rags and drives a smoky old pickup so that he can afford snazzy tackle and go fishing all the time.

When Gierach isn't fishing, or tying flies so he can go fishing again, he is likely to be writing about fishing: writing he does well in *Trout Bum* (1986). Gierach is one of the most entertaining writers about fly fishing for trout to emerge in recent years. All right, so he isn't Sparse Grey Hackle or Robert Traver, nor does he write with the elegance of Tom McGuane, or publish his stuff in *The New Yorker* like Bill Barich. But give him more time: Sparse was in his seventies when *Fishless Days, Angling Nights* was published and Traver in his mid-fifties when *Trout Madness* came out. Gierach is able to combine instruction—in an unobtrusive way—with entertainment. Few can do that. When he is really going good, as in "A Fisher of Small Streams" and "Headwaters" or "Cutthroat Pilgrimage," he vividly evokes the ambience and experience of fishing small mountain streams and the high country.

Gierach probably would agree with the affecting conclusion of an earlier trout bum, Theodore Gordon: "Time flies so fast after youth is past that we cannot accomplish one-half the many things we have in mind, or indeed one-half our duties. The only safe and sensible plan is to make other things give way to the essentials, and the first of these is fly fishing."

Vincent Marinaro, in his *Code*, said that "fly fishing in its best form, in the best circumstances, is a rather secretive and solitary kind of sport." For W.D. Wetherell in *Vermont River* (1984), fly fishing means fishing alone, seeking the solitude that can be soothing or destructive. Robert Traver, Sparse Grey Hackle, and John Gierach usually move with other anglers in their stories, there is dialogue and shared experience. But dialogue for Wetherell is interior; his conversation is with the river.

Wetherell says that he writes fiction for a living but knows no novelists; he loves opera but knows no opera fans; loves trout fishing but fishes alone. After a tussle with words, the solitariness of the river makes him whole again. The price he pays is the lack of shared experience.

Vermont River chapter by chapter records fishing and contemplating the river from winter to winter. Interludes between chapters interrupt the flow for reflections on the study of topographic maps as vicarious fishing in the winter—his substitute for fly tying; boyhood fishing adventures; the relationship of great writers and fishing; an expedition through a Vermont country store where the "good stuff," the fishing tackle, is secluded in back. Literature scholars would call these "digressive intercalary chapters"; intercalary actually works—you could look it up, as Casey Stengel used to say, but I prefer interludes.

Wetherell warns that "little advice will be found here. I am a writer first . . . and the insights I am after have little to do with catching more trout." He writes about his river through the year keeping a whiff of mystery about it, just as he always fishes alone. Companions intrude on mystery. In an expedition to track the river to its source—as a coda to his fishing season—as success is almost at his boots he turns away so that the source of his river remains a mystery.

Robert Traver would have persisted and found an oozy, wet place next to a rural auto graveyard and highway. I do not mean that Wetherell is a solemn writer—he isn't—and the chapter called "My Brilliant Career" recording his three years on the staff of what he calls America's worst fishing magazine or, when a college student, his one day as a clerk in a famous Vermont tackle company matches Traver's humor.

Wetherell's chronicle of a year on his river leaves room for the imagination. Writers need to track feelings to their source, but not necessarily to reveal them. Early in his career, Red Smith interviewed the striptease queen Ann Corio about the secret of her success: "always leave your panties on," she said.

Norman Maclean's *A River Runs Through It* (1976) may not be a trout fishing book but there is a lot of superbly told trout fishing in it. The fishing on the Elkhorn and Big Blackfoot holds the story together and helps to move it along. It's here because it's the best trout fishing fiction (if it is fiction) I have ever read.

Maclean's novella hinges on the intertwined fishing and family relations among the narrator (a stand-in for the author), his brother Paul and their father, his feckless brother-in-law Neal and Neal's family. Paul is a good writer—a reporter on a Montana newspaper—an expert caster and angler, who drinks, fights, and gambles too much. He likes to bet on his fishing and he has made a bet with life that he ultimately loses.

Sparse Grey Hackle said that "the great angler is compounded of terrifically intense concentration and a ferocious, predatory urge to conquer and capture." Paul will risk drowning to get to the best bank to cast from. And after vanquishing a big trout, Paul "with uplifted arm proclaimed himself the victor. Something giant dangled from his fist. Had Romans been watching they would have thought that what was dangling had a helmet on it."

Paul won't be helped whether with a loan of the day's killing fly, or to keep from being killed. Paul's case is classical tragedy, a man yielding inevitably to a fundamental flaw of personality. He is, in a phrase of W.B. Yeats, a "man who loves his destiny." Even though he endangers himself by being behind in the big poker game at Hot Springs, he declines his brother's offer of money or help to get a job on a big newspaper on the West Coast: "I'll never leave Montana . . . And I like the trouble that goes with it."

Maclean is a gifted storyteller; you can't begin without wanting to see how it comes out. He writes simply and directly, one heart to another. Along the way he tells much about what it was like to fish in Montana in the 1930s when the Big Blackfoot was seldom fished, a lost pastoral, where you could sink your beer in the stream to keep it cold and be confident it would be there on your return, and you could catch big trout with two dozen wet flies in your hat.

Maclean writes outward to the common reader and not inward to the trout angler. Most readers of this acclaimed book have not been fly fishers. I have a friend from college days who cares nothing of trout fishing, but who does have three brothers, a sister who died young, and grew up with a more than present father, an army colonel. He read Maclean's book for reasons similar, I believe, to those why Maclean wrote it. Paul's brother, the narrator, said "yet even in the loneliness of the canyon I knew there were others like me who had brothers they did not understand but wanted to help."

When Aldo Leopold's bird dog Gus couldn't find pheasants he pointed meadowlarks. Robert H. Smith grew tired of meadowlarks, of hatchery "rubber" trout, and went on an adventure in search of the real thing: wild, native trout in wild places. The "real thing" didn't merely mean stream-spawned fish, but the original native trout in their ancestral habitat. Smith's quest as recorded in his *Native Trout of North America* (1984) was to find authentic and often "relict" species and subspecies of trout. He would fish for them with the fly only and would keep only those fish needed for photographs.

Smith, trained in biology and geology, retired from the U.S. Fish and Wildlife Service where he was a waterfowl biologist for the Pacific flyway. To prepare for his quest he read all the relevant technical literature and had long conversations with Dr. Robert J. Behnke—an authority of trout on the West. Behnke also checked Smith's manuscript.

Smith's adventure obsessed him nearly full-time for ten years, taking him from the Sierra Madre Occidental of Mexico to the Barren Lands along the Arctic Ocean. Most of his trips to find, fish for, and photograph these native fish were beyond trailheads requiring long hikes or packstrings. On some of them there would be no sign of man "except my own tracks." For Smith these fish were true "symbols of wilderness, true natives . . . the real thing . . . the way it always was."

The geological upheavals of western North America created a multitude of ecological niches resulting in the most varied trout fauna in the world. Trout occur over five life zones from upper Sonoran to Arctic-Alpine. Environmental changes over this vast area resulted in five or six species and twenty subspecies of trout and several species of char. What remains today often are relict populations hanging on in remote headwaters. Even the names suggest wildness: Paiute, Gila, Lahontan, Apache, Redband, Volcano Creek Golden, Mexican Golden, Rio Yaqui.

Smith's search for the authentic was a good idea. His book is an original work, no one had done this before. His is a book of record but it is also an adventure story. For Smith it meant going back in time: a search for the wild and primitive that we share within ourselves. Like a religious pilgrimage, Smith said, "In the process of seeking out the fish I had become a part of it all . . ." Smith reports that "I have still other trout to find, fortunately, to lead me to the high places again. The quest is not over, will never be over." More is going on here, I think, than seeking wild, authentic trout; it is a search for a reconstructed innocence and seeking God in nature. As Datus Proper said, "Innocence is a wild trout."

Are Trout Fishing Books Literature?

So there you have it, the fifteen best trout fishing books of the last thirty years. Inclusion on my list does not mean these books are flawless or that I have no reservations about them—in varying degrees they are not and I do. But this is a time and place for celebration of the best. You may not agree with my choices. Any list of this kind has an element of a game about it, and one of the pleasures such a game affords is the pleasure of disagreement.

Trout fishermen like to point out that fly fishing has the longest and best literature in sport. This notion may be news to enthusiasts of other sports. (Red Smith, for all his love of trout fishing, thought that the best stories in sports were found around racetracks.)

But are trout fishing books literature? If they are or are not, why? What is literature anyway? If the books of entertainment are literature, what of the books of record and instruction?

G.B. Harrison, the eminent Anglo-American scholar of Elizabethan literature, published in 1962 a small book, a sort of testament, called *Profession of English*. Harrison, whose categories I used in this article, divided prose into three groups: prose of record, prose of instruction, and prose of entertainment or delight. He defined literature as having one essential quality: it "must give delight by [its] manner of writing." The chief purpose of prose of delight is entertainment, but, Harrison said, the best prose of record and instruction can also give delight. To be literature, Harrison thought, prose of delight must also possess universality— written outward to the common reader, not inward in a language restricted to a special audience. Consequently, literature must be written so well that it appeals to a wide audience. In my list that includes only Maclean, perhaps Wetherell, and parts of Traver and Sparse Grey Hackle.

137

But is Harrison right? Is giving delight to a wide audience the irreducible nub of literature? And does that mean that nonfiction (such as trout-fishing books) intended for a special readership in a restricted language cannot be literature?

Now comes Terry Eagleton, the polymath and scholar of literature at Oxford. Eagleton argues persuasively in his *Literary Theory, An Introduction* (1983) that literature cannot be defined objectively. We cannot "isolate . . . some constant set of inherent features" in literature. "There is no 'essence' of literature whatsoever." Eagleton declares that "the study of literature is (not) the study of a stable, well-defined entity, as entomology is the study of insects . . ." Eagleton believes that judgments as to what constitutes literature are value judgments and are historically variable because they are socially conditioned.

For example, William Zinsser in his *On Writing Well* said that we are still under the sway of the nineteenth-century definition of literature as novels, short stories, and poetry. But Eagleton said the eighteenth century doubted that "the new upstart form of the novel was literature at all." Annie Dillard in *Living By Fiction* (1982) said that "in two centuries our assumptions have been reversed. Formerly the novel was junk entertainment; if you wanted to write significant literature . . . you wrote nonfiction." Nonfiction we regard today as sincere but artless, she adds. The battleground in the late twentieth century, Zinsser believes, is whether nonfiction can be admitted to the house of literature. He asserts that "nonfiction is where much of the best and most valuable writing (today) is being done." But Zinsser does not reach the issue whether writing well but inward in a restricted language to a special audience can be literature.

G.E.M. Skues published his celebrated *Minor Tactics of the Chalk Stream* in 1910. I am sure that *Minor Tactics* was not considered as literature in 1910 when, as G.B. Harrison said, William Watson, Henry Newbolt, and Alfred Noyes were regarded "as the most promising of modern poets." Who reads Watson, Newbolt, and Noyes today? But Skues is still read. I enjoy re-reading Skues, deriving both pleasure and insight from his several works. (Italo Calvino, the Italian writer, said that you can always tell a classic—no one is ever reading a classic, only re-reading it.) Skues wrote delightfully, but he wrote inward to fly fishermen not outward to a wider audience. Why is Skues not literature when Watson, Newbolt, and Noyes are, even though they are not read anymore?

If a work is written well enough to be appealing to a wider audience, it may be literature. But if a well-written book turns "local," then the boundaries become blurry. Annie Dillard poses the problem: "Among works of nonfiction, which are literature and which are not? Surely there is a distinction between such works as *A River Runs Through It, Green Hills of Africa,* and *Wind, Sand, and Stars* and other nonfiction, from field guides to cookbooks. But where are the boundaries?"

As with many big questions, there may not be an answer.

The Best Trout-Fishing Books Since 1989

Robert H. Berls

Twenty years ago when I began collecting fly-fishing books it was easy to keep up with the new ones. Now fly-fishing books appear incessantly so that keeping up with them threatens to become a full-time job. The proportion of excellent books also increases, it seems to me, as the proportion of sophisticated fly anglers steadily increases. As to the prominence of the latter phenomenon, ask anyone who has regularly fished the western spring creeks, for example, for the last two decades.

Not so long ago you would overhear anglers on, say, Armstrong Spring Creek, announcing that "those light cahills are coming down again." Now they not only know they are pale morning duns, they know the genus and species as well. They no longer "put up" (as the British say) a small conventional light cahill as they used to. Now they will have tied on no-hackles or comparaduns or thorax-ties or be fishing emergers or floating nymphs. The increase in new instructional books reflects and results from the rapid sophistication of anglers and the complexity of angling problems as fishing pressure schools the trout.

The books of introspection about trout fishing, or the distilling of angling experiences into reflective essays, become more frequent too, and they are often well-written. Sometimes this introspection or reflection runs with a search for self. The best writing anywhere is from the writer who writes for himself. James Joyce said that the first question to ask of any work of art is " from how deep a need did it spring?" Right here, someone is likely to bring up Dr. Johnson's famous objection that no one but a blockhead ever wrote except for money. But Johnson lived and wrote before the romantic and modernist movements pulled man's psyche inside out and gave him need for self-analysis and confession. That great modernist, Virginia Woolf, points to the "enormous modern literature of confession and self-analysis." The novelist Anne Lamott in her marvelously instructive and entertaining recent book on writing: *Bird by Bird, Some Instructions on Writing and Life*, says that for a writer "the real payoff is the writing itself." Or as the novelist Jamaica Kincaid said recently in *The New York Times:* "'I'm not writing for anyone at all. . . . I felt compelled to write to make sense of it to myself . . .'"

My charge was to select the best trout-fishing books to appear since the prior review article in 1989. I imposed the same ground rules: no primers, or books on casting or fly tying, or books on salmon or steelhead. Still, there are some awfully good recent fly-tying books out there. I think right away of A.K. Best's *Production Fly Tying* (1989), Gary Borger's *Designing Trout Flies* (1991), Darrell Martin's *Micropatterns, Tying and Fishing the Small Fly* (1994), and Dick Talleur's *The Versatile Fly Tyer* (1990). If I were not excluding the pursuit of anadromy, Sidney Spencer's (an English writer little known in this country) *Fishing the Wilder Shores* (1991) about salmon and sea trout fishing in the west of Scotland and Ireland would be here.

Some other personal favorites are excluded owing to boundary disputes again. Howell Raines's *Fly Fishing Through the Mid-Life Crisis* (1993), an enormously, and deservedly, successful book, covers the fly-fishing waterfront. So does Clive Gammon's *I Know a Good Place* (1989), and E. Donnall Thomas's recent *Whitefish Can't Jump* (1994).

The Favorite Ten: Books of Instruction

The best trout-fishing books usually are written, as Neil Patterson says, by those "who squat on rivers, who haunt them day after day." One thinks of Vincent Marinaro in his photography blind and fishing hut on the Letort Spring Creek, summer evening after evening working out the problems of minute flies or terrestrials or a better dun imitation. Or G.E.M. Skues fishing the Abbots Barton water on the Itchen three days a week for more than fifty years. The hares that Skues started there on the Itchen are still being pursued and with increasing vigor. Or Charles Wetzel in his old farmhouse on Penn's Creek fishing and studying the river and its insects the season through. Or Art Flick, with his beloved Schoharie and its Westkill at his door where he could pop onto them at a moment's need to sort out the problems of identifying their insects and improving imitations for them.

Neil Patterson, in his *Chalkstream Chronicle, Living Out the Flyfisher's Fantasy* (1995), says that fly-fishing and fly-design innovations come from the committed anglers—not the day-trippers. Patterson committed himself twenty years ago to living in a converted stable within earshot of his beat on a Berkshire chalkstream. His passion is tracking the hatches and solving the problems of imitation as the season progresses. His chronicle focuses on fly-design problems and his dissatisfaction with the conventional Halford-originated dry fly: It does not provide what the dry-fly angler needs from it. (Marinaro criticized the Halford dry fly as a conventional wet fly made "vertical." He chastised Skues for not having liberated the dry fly as he did the wet.)

Patterson wanted to design dry flies that were simpler, cheaper, easier to tie, and more successful. The Funneldun design he came up with shows improved floatability, a sharper outline, and a hook-hiding quality since it's an upside-down fly. He believes hiding the hook is important for a dun imitation and critically so for a spinner. It is also a low-riding fly. French market fly fishermen, who caught trout for their livelihood, showed him that when your fly doesn't work up on the surface, get it to sit in the surface.

141

Chalkstream Chronicle is the most entertaining book on fly design since Datus Proper's, and the most absorbing British book on these issues since Goddard's and Clarke's. Neil Patterson joins a short list of contemporary fly-fishing authors who are transforming dry-fly fishing.

Gary LaFontaine, who fishes everywhere and all the time especially in his part of Montana, once described how the Clark Fork of the Columbia was only a measured 248 feet from his office door at the Montana State Prison, enabling him to fish it four or five times a week. His vast experience fishing and guiding and his scuba-diving underwater research into insect emergences and the trouts' perceptions and behavior during hatches are an indispensable dimension to his remarkable theories of dry-fly imitation and attraction developed in his *The Dry Fly: New Angles* (1990).

Although large advances had been made previously in imitation theory, LaFontaine's work has greatly extended it. The problems of imitation for selective, surface-feeding trout are much better understood, and now we know how to create better imitations for selective fish.

LaFontaine's theory of attraction is even more original: No one had developed previously a coherent, field-researched theory of attraction for dry flies. Attraction works best by exciting fish not actively feeding but eager to do so and not zeroed in on a particular insect. These fish take attractors quicker than imitative flies. But which attractor to use? LaFontaine tells you in his provocative book. Using effective attractors extends the time trout will take dry flies, and now that using them is no longer a guessing game for LaFontaine, attractor dry flies are more important than ever to him.

The Dry Fly, New Angles and LaFontaine's previous work, *Caddisflies*, are original, provocative books that demand repeated reading and pondering. LaFontaine has raised our knowledge of caddisflies and dry-fly imitation and attraction to a higher plane. These two books have profoundly reshaped our thinking about fly fishing for trout.

142   In the summer, Gary Borger moves his angling feast out from his early season fishing in Wisconsin to the Rocky Mountain West, and on his spring vacations is off to New Zealand or Tasmania or other angling exotica. Much of the summer he spends fishing the high country lakes and streams on the vast Vermejo ranch in New Mexico. Borger distills his enormous angling experience into his new book, *Presentation* (1995). It's the best and most comprehensive book available on searching for, approaching, and presenting a fly to the trout. A trained biologist, Borger is always analytic and informative in telling you where trout are, and why, in streams and lakes, what they eat and how, and the angling strategies to use. Since the problems of imitation and presentation can't really be separated, the angler should read Borger's *Designing Trout Flies* in tandem with his newer book. The earlier book is useful in solving fly-fishing problems with innovative fly designs (the term that Datus Proper put into the fly-fisher's lexicon) both dry and wet.

The Favorite Ten: Books of Entertainment

John Barsness is that rarity, a Montana trout-fishing author who is a Montana native. In *Montana Time* (1992), he describes the fly fishermen who congregate on the famous Montana rivers to fish the famous hatches as "tourist anglers," but intends no slur. Indeed, he says many of the tourist anglers know an awful lot about catching trout. Barsness, who lives by a trout creek and knows it so well he can sense changes in it without looking at it, says something is missing in all that tourist angling travel. He thinks he knows what it is because he travels a lot for fishing himself. What's missing, he says, is that they don't live by the river in winter, "and that teaches something about trout . . . that all the proficiency in the world cannot."

Barsness begins his book in winter, at ice-out time, arcing the story of his evolution as an angler and blending it with fishing through the seasons. His feeling for the rivers throughout the year is palpable, and he writes perhaps the best description of that seasonal angling apex, the salmon fly hatch, that I have read. But he avoids the famous rivers now, or fishes them at unfamous times, like John Gierach who says he fishes the crowded South Platte at "weird times of the year."

Fishing the "damn good brown trout rivers" of the ranch valleys, Barsness's eyes began to lift "above the hay fields" and he began to climb to the high country for cutthroats and grayling. "That is what grayling are for," he says, "to live in places so pure that people cannot live there . . . with (an) uncompromising innocence." Barsness says "even then I wanted to climb higher" to go into the high country wilderness to pursue trout fishing the way he says it should be: "a lonely occupation."

Barsness has "become enamored of natural systems," of wild trout in wild places. (Datus Proper reminded us that innocence is a wild trout.) Barsness, it seems to me, is searching for innocence as well as wild trout. Americans in one way or another are often searching for innocence, it goes with the territory, to find a shelter from the world or to feel spirit in nature. Barsness's passion for the natural and his humility towards it is the religious temperament.

Montana Time is a gently written, understated, lovely book. Barsness concludes that "there is fly fishing for trout and then there is everything else." That original American trout bum, Theodore Gordon, would have assented to that. *Montana Time* is a small book; I wished it were longer.

Nick Lyons's *Spring Creek* (1992) is the best evocation I know of the experience of fishing a difficult spring creek, day after day, for much of a summer. Lyons places a stream in its setting, so that you know where you are—where he is—and that you are fishing a particular stream in a particular place. Few writers do that. Lyons takes you with him as he crawls to the bank and casts, sitting down, trying not to alert always jittery trout that live in a treeless creek that winds through a sere Serengeti plain under an immense, cloudless sky. Lyons takes you into his

143

mind as he struggles to deceive experienced brown trout during pale morning dun or Western green drake hatches, where with each succeeding day the trout know more and more what their prey looks like through "the skylight on the roof of their world." Lyons tries to learn why a trout took a particular fly and why his new imitation worked better in one part of the creek than another. (As Datus Proper told us about such omnipresent hatches: "The trout learn something about these flies, with hooks or without, and they will tell you. To be sure you are getting the right message, make one small change in your fly between trips.")

There's no shortage of good writing about techniques for fishing the pale morning dun on difficult, flat water, but there is little writing on what it feels like to do it. Nick Lyons shows you. He tells us with Conradian overtones: "Gradually I was traveling deeper into the mystery of it all, traveling with tools that better enabled me to experience what there was to be experienced." Most of our trout streams don't offer such mysteries, but some do and *Spring Creek* is one of them. The accomplished fly fisherman creates order out of confusion, and transforms mystery into art. It's Nick Lyons's best book.

Leonard Wright limits his exploration in his *Neversink, One Angler's Intense Exploration of a Trout River* (1991) to the twelve miles of river he knows intimately, fishing it sixty to seventy days each spring and summer and observing it another thirty to forty days in the off-season. He is as consumed with the challenge of running a fishery as he has been by the fishing itself. *Neversink* is a record of fishing and managing his wild browns and brook trout for well over twenty years. Wright was so absorbed in his fishery that it became a labor of love: he feels guilty if he sneaks off for a day of shad fishing on the nearby Delaware or a week's salmon fishing in Canada.

In the first season on his water, Wright usually knocked on the head the adult trout that he caught, intending them for the skillet. By late summer the fishing on his stretch was lousy. Inquiring whether his riparian neighbors' fishing had held up, he discovered that it had, but he learned also that they seldom killed their trout. Instead of killing his trout, Wright began feeding them.

Neversink is an engrossing record of Wright's experiences feeding his wild trout to get more or larger fish, and of his learning-by-experience habitat improvements. He also details his adventures introducing Canadian-strain brook trout that live longer and grow bigger than the native brookies of the Catskills. Near the end of the book Wright adduces evidence that these Assinicas and Tamiscamies might be catching on. He also describes the state's attempts to assimilate landlocked

Atlantic salmon to this cold river and the reservoir downstream and the hopes and doubts of that venture. Among all the rock-rolling stream improvements Wright, in the interest of leaving no stone unturned, tries managing the invertebrates in his cold, not fertile river, with marginal success.

Roving out from the river, Wright details the valley's flora and fauna and how they interact with the river and its trout. As everywhere, the geology of the region has exerted a dominant influence on the Neversink Valley. (Annie Dillard put it lyrically in her *Teaching a Stone to Talk*: "Geography is life's limiting factor. . . . And if you dig your fists into the earth and crumble geography, you strike geology. The Pacific Ocean, the Negev Desert, and the rain forest in Brazil are local geological conditions. So are the slow carp pools and splashing trout riffles of any backyard creek. It is all, God help us, a matter of rocks.")

Wright loves to fish his river's best hatch, the blue caddis that emerges all of June. He says that on an afternoon in early summer his water on the Neversink is, for him, the best of all possible places to be. Wright's books are always interesting, even absorbingly so, but *Neversink* exceeds them all. When reading it, I just wanted it to go on and on.

In Oregon, Ted Leeson points out in his *The Habit of Rivers, Reflections on Trout Streams and Fly Fishing* (1994), the fishing season never ends. Month after month in that diverse climate and topography, another river, another season, is just reaching its peak. The result, Leeson says, is that he "spends an unseemly amount of time on rivers."

Although his first two chapters are about steelhead and salmon fishing, most of the book isn't in pursuit of anadromy. Leeson describes himself as "in heart or mind, or wherever essences reside, I am a trout fisherman."

Leeson circumnavigates Oregon, by geography and season, fishing around from where it is almost continuously wet to where it seldom rains. He is deft at putting rivers or lakes into their setting; he makes you feel the texture of the place, so that you sniff the misty drizzle in the conifers or taste the grit from the dust devils in the lip-cracking dryness of the high desert.

Leeson isn't pursuing better fly designs or improved techniques. He is after more elusive quarry. He faces obliquely the ultimate questions of why we fish, and why we are so fascinated by rivers. The questions may be unanswerable, but Leeson gives the reader a good first approximation of an answer, as the mathematicians would say. In doing so, Leeson dissolves any pretentiousness about fly fishing, and reduces it to its essence as he sees it.

Any serious angler would be happy to share Leeson's literary journey.

Stranded at night in a jammed, noisy camp-ground on the Deschutes River in stonefly time, Ted Leeson picked his way up through the campers to the canyon rim, and with his big six-cell light sig-naled vainly for the mother ship to beam him up. But Steven Meyers has found his mother ship right here on planet earth in the San Juans of southwestern Colorado.

In *Notes from the San Juans, Thoughts About Fly Fishing and Home* (1992), Steven Meyers tells us why he lives and fishes in the San Juans and could not bear to live anywhere else. Meyers frequently guides on and fishes the big nearby tailwater, the San Juan, and says it is a great place to experiment with flies, sharpen tech-niques, and to work on the details of technical fly fishing. But the tailwaters, even with their large numbers of big trout, lack something for him: a sense of awe or mystery is missing. That is why a tailwater could never be his "home stream," nor could the big Las Animas river where he has lived on its bank for sixteen years, and worries that without special protection its wonderful population of big brown trout will be vulnerable to the increasing number of anglers who are becoming proficient enough to catch them.

A home stream for Meyers has to be a place where you would be surprised to discover you're not alone. So he fishes Lime Creek, and Bear Creek, and other creeks you will never read about.

Meyers isn't certain why trout fishing is so "terribly important" to him, but he suspects it's because the trout is an emblem of the place he has found to be home. It's through this emblem that he begins to understand himself. Meyers likes to spend summers in the high country with horses "tramping about," fishing for trout and looking for gold. Sometimes, he says, instead of filling your hat with nuggets, you fill it "with something other than what you were looking for and that something is even better." Some people after a summer of fishing every day find better flies or better techniques; some people find themselves.

Meyers is an accomplished, graceful writer, one of the best of the fly-fishing essayists who have emerged recently. If you don't already know his writing then try such chapters as "A Hat Full of Gold" or "Drifting" or "Tailwaters and Homewaters" and I think you will agree.

The old men who taught Steven Meyers how to fish for trout didn't know much about modern techniques and knew nothing about the revolutions in fly-tying and rod-making materials, but they did know the streams and the fish. They fished for cutthroats that took a fly unhesitatingly, but would not tolerate splashy casting or careless wading. The old men taught Meyers how to stalk trout and how to present his fly carefully.

The old men who taught the adolescent Harry Middleton to fish for trout in *The Earth Is Enough, Growing Up in a World of Trout and Old Men* (1989) went down to Starlight Creek, that flowed through their hard-scrabble farm in the Ozarks, every day, in every season, as much in search of solace as trout. The creek and the fields and woodlands were not an escape from life for those old men, they were life. Rather than pursuing modern farming techniques and money, they chose to live poor (but not poorly) and decided on trout, quail, and wild turkeys instead of beans. They thought that the world had enough beans but not enough trout or turkeys.

Middleton's grandfather and uncle scorned conventional religion and were seen as atheists in town. They debated and skewered the local clergyman who came weekly for his free dinner. But the passion they showed for their land, and their humility towards it, is the religious temperament. The locals wanted to turn their part of the countryside into an Ozark hillbilly theme park and turn a buck.

Harry Middleton's old men didn't care about the rod materials revolution of their time either. They didn't like glass rods and stuck to their old Phillipson and Winston because glass had a cold, clammy feeling to them. Fiberglass had no grace, Uncle Albert thought. (Marinaro thought that graphite rods "had no soul;" John Gierach, a cane rod addict, described graphite rods as looking "fragile but deadly in the finest tradition of modern technology.")

Elias Wonder, the Sioux Indian and ex-Marine who lived in a shack on the farm, tutored Middleton on fly casting, and told the boy that he was hooked, not the trout, for the trout had him. "Another soul lost," he said "or maybe found." The three old men "heard a music few men cared to hear, music played without end by the natural world . . . they were happy eccentrics." The old men never used bait, only flies, mostly dry flies. They had a code: "'You don't bait what you love. You tempt it, lure it, get under its skin.'"

Harry Middleton was canned from his job as a senior writer for a big magazine publisher not long after *The Earth Is Enough* appeared. He moved to Denver, got a lesser job with a lesser magazine and broke down from severe depression. After being sacked from that job too, for the usual cost-cutting reason, he returned to

Birmingham, worked three menial jobs at once to hold things together and wrote *The Bright Country, A Fisherman's Return to Trout, Wild Water, and Himself* (1993), to show how trout fishing can save your life and your soul. A big, blind Colorado brown trout, a trout raised to mythical proportions, helped to redeem Harry Middleton. (I use mythical in the sense Steven Meyers uses it in *Notes from the San Juans:* not the myth of total fabrication, "but the myth of allowing a fish . . . to achieve poetic, even epic proportions.")

The Bright Country, a very different book from *The Earth Is Enough,* could have been here too. Harry Middleton died from a heart attack, still a young man, shortly after the later book appeared; another casualty of the corporate life. I can't say goodbye to Harry Middleton better than T.H. Watkins did in his review in The Wilderness Society's magazine of *The Bright Country:* "Con Dios, Harry. Good fishing."

I have read all of John Gierach's books and enjoyed them immensely. His books had an immediate attraction for me. There was a falling off a bit, I thought, after *Trout Bum,* but the curve turned up again with *Even Brook Trout Get the Blues* (1992) and *Dances With Trout* (1994). But *Dances With Trout* is not as advertised, since half of its dances are with grouse, deer, snowshoe hares, bass, salmon, and ice-fishing, so *Even Brook Trout Get the Blues* gets the blue ribbon because it has less of such peripheral stuff.

Gierach, as he says, writes about fishing for a living but as a reporter, an observer. He doesn't present himself as a hero-angler and he can be gently self-deprecating: ". . . I tend to envy any fisherman who seems to know what he's doing." He has an easy reading, conversational style that is not as easy to write as it may look. As Anne Lamott says, ". . . how hard it is to make (writing) look effortless."

In *Brook Trout,* Gierach describes how, searching for a place to call home, he moved to a house in the foothills of the Front Range in Colorado with a creek out the door with some trout in it, and felt at home for the first time.

Gierach likes to fish the creeks, the small streams, and writes about it eloquently in his chapter called "Pocket Water." He also likes to wander the high country with an expensive rod, by himself or with others, "to get a taste of things as they really are . . ." as he says in the eponymous chapter.

One reason Gierach fishes the creeks and the high lakes is aesthetic. His first rule is that fishing should be quiet, solitary, and contemplative. (Marinaro thought that fly fishing at its best was that way.) But creeks and high country usually dictate that the trout will be small. He is aware that, as he puts it, "too much horniness for big trout can ruin a fisherman" making him disdain the creeks, but he also admits that the pull of big trout never entirely evaporates. So "if the trout are big enough, rule one can be temporarily suspended" and he joins the crowds on the big waters, the rivers and tailwaters, for the chance at bigger fish and the attractive complexities of technical fishing not usually offered by the creeks. Gierach writes often about the puzzle-solving attractions of technical fishing for experienced fish, but in his casual way he says about midge fishing: "mostly you just need lots of little flies to try."

But when fishing the South Platte, as he writes in "The Hog Hole," where "in the space of an hour or so, fifteen other fishermen tell you the river isn't crowded" it's time to "bag the hog holes" and fish the creeks, high lakes, and beaver ponds where, as Steven Meyers says, "you can be surprised to find that you are not alone."

Reading John Gierach on trout fishing gives you a "taste of things as they really are." I look forward to his next book, for he remains one of the most entertaining trout-fishing writers today.

* * *

149

So there you have it again, the best trout-fishing books since the previous review was written early in 1989. The imitation school retains the high ground of writing about fly fishing for trout. Writing about attractors and presentation has become more analytic and thoughtful as witness the two books included above. Books of reflection and introspection about trout fishing seem to be outpacing instructional books in number, and they are often well-written indeed. Datus Proper once said, "There are a million fly fishermen and half of them are writers." It's beginning to look that way.

Can Fly Fishing Survive the Twenty-first Century?

George Anderson

THE PASSAGE OF FLY FISHING through the twenty-first century will not be as simple a matter as tacking a new calendar up on the wall each year. Fly fishing as we know it today may well be ancient history by the coming century. But by then, the changes probably won't seem dramatic, since the passage of time tends to dissolve vivid memories of the past. I can remember often having a favorite stretch of stream to myself, fishing water that had been untouched that day by other anglers. The trout were larger then too. A three-pound rainbow from the Madison or Yellowstone was considered a nice fish, but four- and five-pound fish were not uncommon either. But the increase in fishing pressure, combined with the lack of quality regulations, hurt the population of larger trout, and the average size of the larger fish dropped by several inches. The discouraging aspect is we're not talking about an evolutionary period of time, just a couple of decades! Multiply this change by a factor of ten, and you will quickly see the dangerous direction the future of fly fishing is taking.

Some might ask why we should even be concerned about the future of fly fishing. Such global problems as overpopulation, starvation, the destabilization that has taken place in Europe and Russia, and AIDS would seem to take precedence over enticing some silly little trout to bite a hook wrapped with fur and feathers. Fly fishing, however, is like the legendary canary in the mine shaft. Fly fishing is a litmus test, if you will, for our environment. If we cannot protect our rivers and fisheries, or strive to make fly fishing a quality experience, our commitment to stewardship has failed.

Increased fishing pressure is one of the major threats to the future of fly fishing. The recent explosion in popularity of fly fishing has resulted in a dramatic increase in fishing pressure, especially on the most popular public waters. There are frighteningly few premier fly-fishing waters in the world left, and this finite number is decreasing daily due to natural and man-made disasters as well as the systematic destruction of the surrounding environment by those more concerned about jobs and wealth than the protection of our trout streams or the surrounding environment.

Along with the dramatic increase in numbers of anglers has come an overall degradation of the fly-fishing experience. Ironically, much of the fishing pressure results from regulations, like slot limits or catch-and-release, designed to protect fisheries. Because these regulations have dramatically improved the fishing on many rivers, scores of fly fishermen seek out these more highly regulated streams and rivers.

Certainly, this has been the case in Montana on famous rivers like the Madison and Bighorn. Thirty years ago, when I started floating the Madison, fishing the famous salmon fly hatch, you might have seen twenty boats floating a given stretch of water on any day. Now it is common to count eighty boats a day on this same stretch. If you are the first boat down the river that morning you'll find some cooperative trout and uncongested water to fish, but if you are the seventy-fifth boat, the trout are getting shellshocked and not nearly as anxious to take a fly. Fishermen floating ahead of you have pulled their boats out and are wade fishing the best water, so you won't be able to jump out of the boat anywhere you like and fish your favorite pool.

The Bighorn in recent years is a good example of fishing pressure running rampant. The river has experienced some extremely heavy fishing pressure, especially during the late summer months when the river is low, insect hatches are prolific, and dry-fly fishing is at its peak. The Bighorn's reputation as perhaps the finest trout stream in the country with good public access adds to the frenzy. Fishing pressure from wade and float fishermen can be so heavy in prime time that I've floated 3 to 4 miles at a time without finding a single place to pull over to do some wade fishing, without encroaching on other anglers. Times like these make you feel like throwing in the towel and saying, "To hell with it. This kind of fly fishing just isn't worth the trouble."

Fly fishermen are drawn to the sport largely because of the solitude it can offer. Difficulty in finding a decent piece of water to fish or having problems with other fishermen can quickly ruin your day. On congested rivers like the Bighorn, proper fishing etiquette often takes a backseat to obnoxious tactics fishermen and guides use to tie up their favorite water. Unpleasant confrontations occur, with anglers and sometimes even guides yelling at one another. Inattentive boat fishermen will drift toward you, putting down your school of rising fish. Often other fly fishermen are just ignorant, or have perhaps dismissed some of the most basic rules of fishing etiquette. Even fly-fishing neophytes know that it's not proper to walk right into a pool and fish the water in front of a fellow angler, but today on these crowded streams anglers and guides are pulling sophisticated stunts that tread squarely in the gray area—or beyond the fringe of acceptable fishing etiquette.

On the spring creeks, with fish everywhere and plenty of good water to fish, an angler often will sit in one spot all day so that he won't have to give up his favorite pool to another fisherman. On the Bighorn, guides are getting their clients on the water at 6 A.M., rowing downriver to stake out their favorite piece of water, then waiting hours for the good hatches to start, and the fish to start rising. Some of these guides work the very same water every day, making it nearly impossible for anyone else to fish these prime pools.

On waters where other anglers are often only a stone's throw away, one needs to be especially conscious of fishing etiquette, and how his actions will affect or offend fellow anglers. If, at the end of the day, you can say that you haven't encroached on other anglers, put their fish down, or somehow fouled up their fishing, it's been a good day of fly fishing.

In the future, fly fishing on many well-known public waters will become less of a quality experience unless unprecedented changes take place. Fly fishermen seeking less congested angling will have to revert to fishing private water, often paying a fee to fish. Others will have to exchange solitude for larger fish. Many experienced fly fishermen seek out lesser-known waters, content to scale down their

tackle and catch smaller fish if it means that they will have the stream to themselves. The measure of a good day of fly fishing isn't just the catch, it's also the
enjoyment of the outdoors in a beautiful, uncrowded setting, and the camaraderie
of friends.

Without any regulation on fishing pressure, future public waters will become
a zoo of inconsiderate, intolerant fly fishers threatening the very existence of the
fly-fishing values we hold so sacred. Even in the near future, the only waters where
one will still be able to find larger fish and pursue that "quality experience" may
be on private water, where the angler must pay a fee but where the numbers of fly
fishermen are carefully matched to each stretch of water. Such is the case today in
England and across most of Europe. Free public fishing is a thing of the past
unless you are after "rough" fish like chubs and carp.

It's sad to think that in the future, high-quality fly fishing will only be found
on private water, available only for the wealthy. But it doesn't have to be this way
if people are willing to accept some level of control that would protect the fishing
environment and also enhance everyone's fishing experience. The federal government and state agencies are currently attempting to regulate access and fishing
pressure on some rivers, such as the Colorado River through the Grand Canyon
and the Smith River in Montana, where the sole access is on state or national forest land. By limiting daily launches, these agencies closely control boating and
fishing pressure on these rivers, which results in a quality experience for everyone.

State fish and game departments need to find ways to limit fishing access on
the most crowded streams and rivers. Management plans can be designed for
overly crowded rivers with operational costs funded by anglers paying a fee for
daily rod rights. Fly fishermen would make reservations in advance, much as they
do on the privately owned Montana spring creeks like Armstrong's, Nelson's, and
DePuy's. The remaining available space could be set aside on a first-come, first-
served basis.

I dream of a plan like this, but of course it's about as likely to happen as
Atlantic salmon running up the Yellowstone. I've seen it all before. Greed enters
the equation and decimates the best-laid plans. At the Fish and Game hearings,
everyone would be screaming at the commissioners, wanting their little piece of
the pie. No one would be willing to compromise. Outfitters and guides wouldn't
want any limitations on the numbers and makeup of outfitters on the river or how
many guides they could run each day. Nonfishing pleasure boaters just out to float
and drink beer or paddle their kayak would scream bloody murder. Private land

owners along the river wouldn't stand for being told they could fish only certain days. Threats of lawsuits would unfold and the state agencies would drop the whole issue like a hot potato!

But without some kind of limitation on the number of fishermen on these crowded waters, conflicts arise. Fly fishermen seeking more than catching a lot of big fish leave these streams. Ironically, the people that are left to fish these waters are often the most obnoxious and have the least regard for fishing etiquette.

Waters where a quality fly-fishing experience is likely to survive are in our national parks. The National Park Service is well aware of the effects of population pressures on our environment and has taken steps to limit the number of campers, hikers, and fishermen when specific natural resources are being overused. For instance, limits are imposed on the number of daily visitors to parks like Yosemite. In Yellowstone Park, the number of campsites has been reduced in many areas, and strict limitations have been imposed on backcountry use by both outfitters and private individuals. Unfortunately, the park service has not regulated the number of anglers on any given stream and at times the fishing pressure has increased to objectionable levels on some streams such as the Firehole, Madison, and the Yellowstone above the falls. Even backcountry streams open to daily use like upper Slough Creek have experienced a noticeable increase in fishing pressure just in the past ten years. Overnight camping on many backcountry streams like Slough Creek is limited to a few existing campsites and these are tightly controlled by the Park Service, which in turn effectively moderates fishing pressure.

155

Most fly fishermen are reluctant to hike more than a mile or so to get to their fishing, so most of these backcountry streams in Yellowstone and other parks will not face the more immediate problems of heavy fishing pressure.

Unlike rivers such as the Madison or Bighorn, which run through both public and private lands, waters inside national parks can be regulated with relative 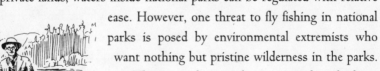 ease. However, one threat to fly fishing in national parks is posed by environmental extremists who want nothing but pristine wilderness in the parks.

These people consider even catch-and-release fishing to be unacceptable. Fishermen are seen as upsetting a fragile environment by wading in the streams, stressing trout or spooking wild animals such as elk and moose that graze along the waterways. Fishermen also present potential conflicts with endangered species such as the grizzly bear, and for this reason some of Yellowstone Park's waters are currently closed to any fishing. Perhaps these national park waters will remain a model for the preservation of large wild trout and a unique fly-fishing experience.

The destruction of fish habitat and reduced water quality also pose major hurdles for the survival of fly fishing. Organizations like Trout Unlimited and the Federation of Fly Fishermen have been instrumental in launching projects to improve trout streams, with the goal of perpetuating quality fly fishing as well as protecting the environment. Nevertheless, many of our finest waters are feeling the long-term effects of pollution or dewatering that could spell the death knell for these great streams.

Pollution has many ugly faces. It's not only the obvious pollution from chemical spills or industrial waste that gets into our trout streams, but also more subtle types of pollution like silt pollution or the leaching of drain fields into our river systems. In many resort areas, there is unregulated building close to rivers and streams, and the resultant long-term pollution problems are just now becoming evident. Summer homes, which are often built close to the floodplain, depend on septic systems and drain fields. Homeowners and builders often don't consider the ramifications of the failure of these systems or the cumulative long-term effects of discharges into aquifers and groundwater table. Nutrients and phosphates added to these systems affect pH levels and can be just as devastating as acidic or metallic discharge from mining activities. As a result, aquatic vegetation can change rapidly, often threatening insect populations. Insects like stoneflies and mayflies, primary trout food, are often the first to be affected.

Indiscriminate use of fertilizers, insecticides, and weed killers have tragic results, degrading overall water quality and, in some instances, causing severe fish mortality. In the West, little attention has been paid to the long-term effects of these farming practices on our rivers and streams.

Years ago I found a beautiful little spring creek that held a lot of large fish—big browns which ran up into the creek from one of our major rivers and found the perfect balance of superior habitat, abundant food, and ideal spawning conditions. We often found these three- to five-pound browns in the deeper bends the spring creek had created as it meandered through a meadow on its course to join the larger river. Where there was deeper holding water and good cover we would find big fish. There was enough gradient and current speed between some pools to find a good gravel bottom that provided ideal spawning habitat and a nursery for the younger trout. We became friends with the rancher and he gave us permission to fish. Of course, my friend and I vowed to keep our little stream a secret, and since it was off the beaten track, few other fishermen discovered it.

Things changed sooner than we would have ever thought. The cattle market was down and our rancher friend was looking to supplement his income by raising some wheat up on a big bench of land overlooking the meadow and spring creek. Early that spring he plowed the land and put in a pumping station on the spring creek, which would push water up a half mile to a big pivot sprinkler on the bench. The wheat crop flourished, but this was the beginning of the end for the fishery. The fertilizers the rancher used were carried back into the spring creek with the irrigation water, and within a couple of months, the weed growth in the spring creek had increased tenfold. Even the deep pools and undercut banks in the stream bends were soon choked with algae growth we had never seen before. It became impossible to find open water to fish, much less find any of the big brown trout. With the algae choking the water flow and spreading it out, the deeper channels and bends filled in with silt. By the late fall none of the big fish were able to run into the creek to spawn as they had in the past. With all the weed growth they simply couldn't navigate the stream to get to the headwaters where they had spawned in past years. Even if they could have somehow gotten through, silt now covered the gravel beds where these big browns spawned in the past. It was over. Our wonderful little stream had changed so dramatically that the following spring we could hardly recognize the pools we used to fish. Five years after the farmer developed the bench and planted his wheat, he was bankrupt and sold the ranch. The damage had been done and today, nearly ten years later, the stream is still badly silted but slowly returning to its natural state. The browns haven't yet returned, but without the wheat, fertilizer, and pesticides at least there is hope.

Silt pollution in our streams and rivers has more recently been recognized as one of the primary reasons for the destruction of trout habitat. Silt washed into streams can build up over time, threatening insect populations that depend on clean gravels for their existence. Excessive silt can decrease water depth and eliminate deeper channels in smaller streams, severely limiting the habitat for larger fish. Silt pollution that occurs during the time when trout are spawning can cut off the flow of clean water over the eggs, substantially reducing the number of fry that will survive.

Silt pollution is often the result of mismanaged logging operations. Clear-cutting vast tracts of timber without regard for the headwaters of rivers is one obvious source. There will be many battles fought in the future to protect our old-growth forests of the West and Northwest, and the outcome will have a direct bearing on the future of high-quality trout fishing in these river systems. While our national forest systems do have some control over logging operations on federal lands, a great deal of logging is done on private land, where there are few limitations on timber harvest or regulations for erosion control. Other major sources of silt pollution include commercial and residential building, and highway construction.

Fortunately, environmental impact statements are now required for many large development projects. Water quality is of primary concern to everyone today, and various state agencies, as well as environmentally conscious organizations like Trout Unlimited, are making developers aware of the legal consequences of degrading water quality.

Overgrazing or bad grazing practices also have come into focus as a primary source of silt pollution. Cattle and other livestock have traditionally been given unlimited access to the land, and the resultant damage caused to streams and rivers is dramatic, especially over time. The damage is particularly noticeable on smaller streams, where livestock eat down the vegetation along the banks and cause an enormous amount of silt pollution by breaking down the banks and wading through the middle of the streams. Projects by private landowners to fence off most of the streambanks and allow access for livestock only at certain points have been very successful in improving the stream environment and fishery. Fishing clubs and other organizations have undertaken many of these projects, providing the manpower and funds to help landowners improve streams. This is expensive work and it makes sense for us to find new ways to help farmers and ranchers participate in these programs. Funding on a federal level or some form of tax relief could provide the needed incentive.

Another significant factor in the survival of fly fishing for trout is the amount of water itself. In the past there was plenty of water for everyone—farming and ranching interests as well as cities and commercial development. Today there is a critical shortage of water. Larger rivers have felt the ill effects of a reduction in flow, and many reservoirs and smaller streams are drained dry to satisfy demands for water. Growth of larger cities has placed further demands on the availability of water, often from headwaters of rivers hundreds of miles away.

The future of trout fishing depends on our ability to formulate a plan that will protect minimum stream flows in all of our rivers and streams. Such a plan would allow state agencies like fish and game departments as well as environmentally conscious organizations to buy water rights from landowners and then to keep water flowing on a constant, year-round basis to protect streams and rivers. Water rights are the key to the equation, and have been the source of bitter battles in the past. As incredible as it may seem, until recently fishing was not even considered a beneficial use of water in Montana. Ranching, farming, and other commercial interests, as well as cities and towns, had the right to every drop of water. Many smaller streams that could be wonderful fishing are sucked bone dry in the summer months when all the available water is rerouted off into fields to flood irrigate water-intensive crops.

Recently, state fish and game departments have been able to get some minimal reservations for instream flows on larger streams and rivers. Next, we must somehow devise a means of promoting and protecting minimal flows in our smaller streams. Farmers and ranchers are utilizing more efficient methods of watering crops today than in the past, when they relied almost entirely on gravity-flow flood irrigation. Large pivot and wheelline irrigation systems are proving to be more cost-efficient but more importantly, use a lot less water than was needed in the past. As a result, excess water is available to remain in streams for the protection of trout and the aquatic environment.

159

I believe fly fishing will survive its passage through the twenty-first century. Complex variables will force changes, but all is not gloomy on the horizon. In my view, fly fishing will be seen as an integral part of a greater plan to save our environment for future generations. Many people today have a greater concern than ever before about protecting the environment, even if they are not fishermen. And there is a growing realization that our environment is already in trouble and must be protected in order for us to survive.

Who Says They Don't Make
Trout Streams Anymore?

William O. McLarney

AT FIRST ALL WE WANTED to do was fix a trout stream. That was our goal: "trout, trout, trout," recalls Mike Arritt. Mike is one of the stalwarts of the Cape Cod Chapter of Trout Unlimited, which must have set some sort of record by logging 15,500 hours of volunteer labor (so far) toward restoration of the Quashnet River. In the process they have rediscovered the hoary environmental adage that "Everything is hitched together."

The stream-fixers have found themselves dealing, not only with trout habitat, but with wildlife, marine issues, open space concerns, drinking water and Indian land rights. Though most chapter members would never have dreamed it when the project began in 1975, they have become the spearhead of a 7,600-member coalition forcefully raising the question: "Where does the development of Cape Cod stop?" Not just with sportsmen and environmentalists, but with the business community, in the political arena and in the consciousness of the general public.

The environment which most immediately concerns the Cape Cod TUers stands out on the map as the largest "empty spot" on the Cape. It is the Quashnet River–Waquoit Bay watershed, shaped like an hourglass and just as full of sand. The upper bulb of the glass is the Quashnet basin, 7.5 square miles of mostly open space, within which innumerable cold springs combine to form a small but deep stream of freshwater with water quality unsurpassed in the crowded Northeast. The lower bulb is the semi-closed Waquoit Bay complex, where Quashnet trout fatten on shrimp and mummichogs. Like the Quashnet Valley, Waquoit Bay is, by Northeastern standards, an unusually pristine environment. Connecting the two "bulbs" is the 0.8-mile intertidal portion of the Quashnet, known locally as the Moonakis River. Here the Quashnet watershed narrows to a width of 1,000 feet. As we shall see, a healthy Moonakis is as critical to the functioning of the Quashnet-Waquoit system as an unobstructed passage to a real hourglass.

By way of analogy, the history of the Quashnet fishery might be described as having a similar shape. At one end is a glorious past when the Quashnet supported a naturally reproducing "salter" brook trout fishery along its entire four-mile length and in Waquoit Bay, too. During this century, the fishery has been squeezed down almost, but not quite, to nothing. Today, the sands of the Quashnet are moving, literally and figuratively, toward an expanding future with the historic fishery restored.

The narrow point in the historical hourglass was reached just prior to 1975, as the culmination of centuries of environmental abuse which began when the first Englishman took an axe to the climax forest which once covered inland Cape Cod. By 1820, the Cape was essentially deforested. Next came the mill dams, which blocked off almost every major Cape stream. The freshwater brook trout fishery persisted, but the fat, silvery salters all but disappeared.

The alewives and the blueback herring which fed both men and trout were less fortunate, and occasioned an early environmental protest, culminating in the Falmouth "herring war" of 1800. One individual, whether in protest against blockage of the rivers or the radical ideas of the conservationists of his day is not clear, "conceived the idea of loading one of the old cannon on the [Falmouth] Green with herring. The charge was tamped down, the gun rammed to the muzzle with herring, and the match applied. The gun burst, probably from steam or gas generated by the unusual charge, and killed the gunner."

Damming was only a prelude to the major assault on the Cape's streams, launched by the cranberry industry in 1895. While cranberry bogs may be as integral to postcard New England as lighthouses, they can be environmental disasters, particularly along major streams.

To construct a cranberry bog, the stream must be straightened and turned into a ditch, with the sole function of regulating water supply. Tributary ditches are dug at right angles. A series of small dams is constructed, for the bog must be flooded in winter to prevent freezing of the roots. Perhaps worst of all, the natural vegetation must be cut and a layer of sand spread over the entire surface. Of course, part of the sand washes off, burying and sterilizing the stream's natural gravel bed and necessitating annual replenishment of sand. Later, pesticides and herbicides were added to the list of insults. By World War I, the entire length of the Quashnet Valley had been converted to what was touted as "the world's longest cranberry bog."

As bad as the bogs had been, their abandonment in the 1950s was worse. At first, with the cessation of sanding and spraying, there was a period of respite. The Massachusetts Division of Fisheries and Wildlife purchased 26 acres of riverside land, comprising roughly a mile and a quarter of the valley, and established a fishery based on hatchery brook trout. But now a shrub known as sweet gale took over the bogs. First it crept up the edge of the river. Then it arched over the water, drooped and fell into the stream, causing it to overflow its banks. The sodden banks crumbled, widening the stream and adding tons of sand and silt to the streambed. TU's early brush cutting sessions had an almost paleontological air, as layer after layer of brush, deposited over 20 years, came up.

As of 1975, though the mill dam and most of the cranberries were long gone, the Quashnet was what one TUer described as "prime white sucker habitat," with a few trout hanging on (about one per 100 feet, according to electrofishing estimates). Even those few trout were unfishable; to negotiate the Quashnet involved hunkering through a tunnel of sweet gale laced with greenbriar, all the while chest-deep in ice-cold mud. The banks were, as TU project leader Francis H. Smith put it, "like a floating bowl of Jell-O." The "river" was often literally invisible.

Nature might have restored the Quashnet and the salter fishery, given a few centuries, except that development would have gobbled it up. Besides, the Trout Unlimited gang didn't want to wait that long to cast a fly—though it sometimes appears that they, or their great-grandchildren, may work that long on the Quashnet.

Aquatic Biologist Joseph Bergin of the Division of Fisheries and Wildlife played a major role in the next step. His particular interest was the sea-run brown trout fishery, which had been established on the Cape beginning in the 1960s, and had produced fish of up to 12 pounds from rivers like the Coonamessett, the Childs, the Mashpee, the Santuit, the Marston's Mills, Scorton Creek and their estuaries. It is difficult fishing, but the possibility of hooking salmon-sized trout in streams which average perhaps 15 feet in width is enough to set any angler's pulse to racing.

For all of its problems, the Quashnet had the best water quality of any of the Cape streams; Bergin wanted to use it as a source of broodstock for a project being carried out at the nearby East Sandwich hatchery. The idea was to use Quashnet spawners as the basis for developing an anadromous strain of brown trout adapted and keyed to Cape Cod streams. There were two obstacles: Bergin could scarcely get his shocker into the Quashnet, and the larger spawner browns couldn't get past a stopped-up culvert at Martin Road, just a few hundred yards above tide-water.

So Bergin enlisted the help of the TU chapter, with the initial goals of unplugging the Martin Road culvert and cutting 800 feet of the stream-choking brush just above it. To Bergin's amazement, once the TU crew got involved, "They just wouldn't quit." The weekend project evolved into a major restoration effort.

The project was first described for *Trout* readers in 1979 by Thomas R. Pero, who enthused, "To date the chapter has invested an incredible 4,000+ man-hours." At that time no one thought the effort would pass its first decade still going strong and looking to quadruple the figure which astounded Pero. Today, everyone acknowledges that the project is not quite completed. Mike Arritt, with something between a grimace and a mischievous grin, opines, "We'll be cutting brush for the next ten years."

Cutting brush—no non-combatant who has heard talk of instream structures, selective breeding, tree planting and all the other glamorous components of the Quashnet project can imagine the sheer amount of cold, sloppy drudgery the TU crew has put in fighting old sweet gale. Getting rid of the pesky shrub is the key to firming the Quashnet's quaking banks, to flushing the cranberry industry's sand down through the Moonakis and out to sea, and to making the river fishable.

Trouble is, sweet gale grows back, but the project is gaining on it. Part of the key to ultimate victory is to cut the shoots in the fall, just before the plant goes dormant. Cutting is followed by planting reed canary grass. While some have criticized the project for introducing an exotic plant, its role is to stabilize the banks so as to make way for native grasses—and for the 1,100 trees so far planted by the chapter. Today, in the upper portion of the 1.25-mile project area, the banks are as firm as when Indians roamed the Quashnet Valley, and the TU crew is talking about re-establishment of native wildflowers.

Eliminating brush "undams" the river and allows it to cleanse itself, but TU has aided the process by installation of deflectors to concentrate the current where it is most needed. These were described in Pero's 1979 article, but in the interim the project has spawned an innovation: the temporary deflector. Made of boards tacked to vertical posts and set in the stream bottom—but not covered or backfilled—the temporary deflector is used to help the river eliminate discrete patches of sand and sediments. The assumption is that, with the stream stabilized in its natural channel, cleaned areas will continue to be self-flushing, and the deflector can be uprooted for use elsewhere. Two people can construct and set a temporary deflector in one and a half hours, versus one hundred hours of labor to construct the permanent sort.

Other activities which have occupied the crew's time are construction of overhead cover for the trout, re-establishment of the herring run, and persuading the state to designate the Quashnet a catch-and-release fishery (a custom already long honored by chapter members). The overhead covers, approximating undercut banks, have been highly successful, but nature has done even better. Opening up the river to sunlight stimulated the growth of aquatic plants like water starwort, and now there are perhaps more trout under this natural cover than under the TU structures.

Next to brushcutting, the most onerous task has been cleaning out the small ditches which connect the Quashnet Valley's myriad springs to the river. This involves crawling on hands and knees through an icy trickle, scooping semi-liquid black organic mud into a bucket (for ultimate use in sodding overhead covers). But no one really minds. Not only is the icy water a constant reminder of why we are all here, but the ditches are the favored habitat of wild brook trout fingerlings.

Though the project is unfinished, the chapter's initial goal of "trout, trout, trout" has been realized. The twenty-fold increase reported in the 1979 article for the first stream section has been replicated throughout the project area, and both species are reproducing on the newly exposed gravel. The shocker has turned up browns of up to 10 pounds, and last September chapter member Matt Patrick gleefully told me of taking a fat, silvery 14-inch brookie—a salter? In that same month I walked downstream along the Quashnet with my wife and daughter, not fishing, not stalking, just showing them the progress. The sound of feeding trout was as insistent as the chittering of the chickadees.

Not only is the Quashnet well on its way to restoration as a fishing stream, the former impenetrable tangle is giving way to an aesthetic triumph which is also prime wildlife habitat. For Mike Arritt, "The beauty of this is, this is public property. Anyone who wants to go down there and use it, walk around, can—you don't have to be a fisherman to enjoy the river. It's a tremendous place to go and just to be."

As chapter members became increasingly aware that their efforts benefited more than trout and trout fishermen, others were becoming more aware of TU; just in time, for the river is threatened anew, and the battle is too big for TU to fight alone.

One of the major environmental and political issues in Barnstable County (Cape Cod), the nation's second fastest growing county, is preservation of open space and, once TU's efforts made it possible to enter and leave the Quashnet Valley unscarred and unmuddied, it became clear that the river and its environs constituted an extraordinarily valuable open space parcel. That there is so much open space remaining in Mashpee, one of two towns through which the Quashnet flows, is largely due to the Wampanoag Indians, who tied up development for years with a controversial land suit. The Indians, distrustful of anything that smacks of officialdom, have remained aloof from the TU project for most of its duration. But, as development closes in, they increasingly view TU's conservation goals as consistent with their philosophy of land use, and have become valuable allies.

An issue which fires up even more of the Cape Cod citizenry than open space is groundwater. Plainly stated, there is not enough to go around, and much of what there is, is contaminated.

The entire Cape draws from a single source aquifer, replenished only by the rain which falls on the 400 square miles of sandy soil between Bourne and Provincetown. In effect, all the Cape's 150,000 citizens and its many more annual visitors have their straws in the same bucket, a bucket increasingly clouded by toxic wastes, pathogenic bacteria, salt-water intrusion, and just plain depletion. As it happens, the Quashnet is perched atop one of the last untapped and uncontaminated portions of that aquifer, a fact not lost on many people who may care little for trout, but yearn for a good drink of water.

Who Says They Don't Make Trout Streams Anymore?

Freshwater anglers constitute a tiny minority of the Cape's resident and transient population, but nearly everyone uses the sea. Several hundred people still engage in commercial fishing. Sport fishing, swimming and boating are all vital to the local economy. In an area where marine pollution is a growing concern, Waquoit Bay has been one of the bright spots. With the exception of the old and densely populated Seacoast Shores Development on the west side of the bay, both its shorelines and its watershed have been relatively undeveloped, and water quality and marine fishery data reflect that fact.

Yet lately Waquoit Bay has shown signs of eutrophication, and some scientists have referred to it as a "mini-Chesapeake." In recent years high coliform counts have caused Health Department closures of Waquoit Bay shellfish beds for the first time. Examination of a series of aerial photos taken from 1938 to the present shows the once extensive eelgrass beds of the eastern bay being reduced to a few small patches. Meanwhile, filamentous algae and dead eelgrass have combined to form a three-foot-deep layer of gunk on the bottom in the middle of the bay. These bottom waters are already close to "dead" and there is the danger that some summer most of the bay will go anoxic.

The single largest contributor of freshwater to the bay—as well as the cleanest—is the Quashnet. Further freshwater input comes from Childs River, Red Brook and a few smaller streams, but most of the rest enters as groundwater, seeping in around the edges or under the bay. And that groundwater is increasingly contaminated by sewage from old, failing tanks and nutrients from new sewage treatment systems.

The current focus of development activity in the Waquoit Bay watershed is the high ground on both sides of the Moonakis. There, in the neck of the hourglass, is where water quality is poorest and shellfish closures most frequent. Were the Moonakis to go anoxic, it would constitute a barrier to sea-run trout. A stop-gap solution might be to increase tidal flushing by relieving a bottle neck where a narrow bridge and causeway constrict the Moonakis at Meadow Neck Road. But sooner or later the issue of water quality in Waquoit Bay must be confronted.

Waquoit Bay is not without advocates. Much of its pristine character is due to the efforts of Citizens for the Protection for Waquoit Bay (CPWB), a group that emerged in response to "insurmountable opportunity" around 1981, and persuaded the state to invest five million dollars in purchasing the 432-acre South Cape Beach, which guards the southeast corner of the bay, and uninhabited 332-acre Washburn Island, which shields the bay proper from Seacoast Shores. As of

1986, CPWB seemed to have outlived its usefulness, until the bay met a new threat, and Citizens met Trout Unlimited.

The threat, as ever, was development. In 1986 TU had urged the Massachusetts Department of Environmental Management to purchase a 255-acre piece on the west side of the river just above the project area. An outfit known as Forward Development Corporation (FDC) spent 3.2 million dollars to outbid the state, and purchased an additional 130 acres east of the river. They then announced plans to build 570 condominium units along Route 28, virtually on the river's edge and just above the Moonakis. Mashpee had passed an open space ordinance which would require FDC to donate part of the land to the town for conservation use, but TU members and other conservationists realized that was not enough.

No matter how well sewage from the development was treated, it would add to nutrient loading in the river and bay. Not to mention wear and tear on the river from an urban density population.

The problem called for more money and more voices than TU could muster. Just then, opportunity knocked. In June 1986, Chapter Secretary Linda M. Golder called then Chapter President Matt Patrick. She and her husband, Bob, had been talking with CPWB chairman Henry Dick. CPWB was suffering from "total burnout" and was looking to disband and donate their remaining funds to a worthy cause. A meeting was arranged with Patrick, the Golders, TU Chapter Vice President Brian E. Tucholke, and the CPWB board. TU didn't want the money, they wanted the organization. Presto—the *ad hoc* Quashnet Coalition was formed, with TU and CPWB as charter members. Matt took the CPWB presidency, and Brian moved up to be TU Chapter President.

"So far as I know, I don't think TU ever built a coalition before in Massachusetts, but it wasn't very difficult at all. We had the issues and they were good ones," explains Fran Smith.

With two organizations counted in, Patrick and Tucholke went after more.

In Falmouth, the 300 Committee, formed to purchase open space in commemoration of the town's tricentennial, joined and has provided funds to hold key pieces of property.

The Association for the Preservation of Cape Cod joined and has facilitated mailings to a membership which has so far grown to 7,600.

In Mashpee, a Voter Information Association has been formed, and elected its candidates to town office by campaigning around the drinking water issue. They saw the protection of the Quashnet Valley as key to their future and joined. At one stroke a substantial percentage of the population of Mashpee was in the coalition.

Although the Wampanoags had fundamental differences with the towns on the water question, Patrick lobbied council president Joan Tavares and chief Earl Mills, and the Mashpee Wampanoag Tribal Council came on board, confirming their oft-stated dedication to wildlands conservation.

Rod and gun clubs, yacht clubs, concerned individuals—everyone was joining. In the latter category a number of scientists at the nearby Marine Biological Laboratory (MBL) and Woods Hole Oceanographic Institution (WHOI) would be key.

Through an effort involving scientists like WHOI's Dr. John Teal (coauthor of the classic *Life and Death of the Salt Marsh*), CPWB member Don Bourne and others, Waquoit Bay had been designated a National Estuarine Research Reserve. Although the Federal statutes governing this little known category of "protected" area are virtually toothless, the designation has drawn positive attention and research funding.

One of the most exciting studies has been initiated by MBL biologist Dr. Ivan Valiela. According to scientists like Teal and Valiela, the public often fails to distinguish between the sort of organic pollution that causes high bacteria counts and closure of shellfish beds and swimming areas, and nutrient loading, which is less noticeable—until there is a fish kill. Of the two, Teal says, "I stress nutrient loading because, in theory at least, there is a technical solution to pathogens." (Proper sewage treatment.)

Valiela opines that the big question is this: "Nutrients are being accumulated in vegetative tissues. Does this mean that one day everything will go anoxic?" (When that vegetation dies off.) Valiela and his graduate students are starting to look at things like the eelgrass die-off and algal blooms, and relate them to nutrient input. According to Valiela, "All previous studies of loading are back-of-the-envelope guesses, with errors of an order of magnitude due to extrapolation from, say, Long Island." As a result of their Waquoit Bay studies, Valiela's group eventually hopes to be able to predict the impact of building one more subdivision or one more house.

The importance of this work has not been lost on Trout Unlimited, and the local chapter has contributed $1,000 as seed money toward a larger National

Science Foundation grant for Valiela's work. The grant—from an organization of freshwater anglers to a marine scientist who may never see a trout during the course of his work—is public acknowledgment that everything is hitched together. Clean groundwater makes the Quashnet work as a trout stream, and Waquoit Bay work as an estuary. Contaminate the Quashnet and you push Waquoit Bay toward the brink. Clean up Waquoit Bay and you enhance the Quashnet. Protect the groundwater and you save it all. And the way to protect groundwater is to control what happens on the land—including in the Quashnet watershed.

So, with marine research and stream restoration in good hands, the Quashnet Coalition set out to protect as much land as they could in the Quashnet/Waquoit watershed, beginning with the FDC property. Given the outrageous real estate prices on Cape Cod, the coalition had to turn to state government.

There they found a friend in upper Cape Representative Tom Cahir. Cahir, a non-angler, already realized that "as a consequence of the Cape's being a sole source aquifer, we have to grasp every way to thwart development." Attendance at a TU meeting convinced him that this particular effort to stem development had national significance, and he agreed to sponsor House Bill 5014, the Quashnet Bill, seeking $10 million to buy out FDC.

The Quashnet Coalition organized a phenomenally successful letter-writing campaign. Though it might be called a local issue, the Quashnet Bill produced more mail than any other issue before the Massachusetts legislature in recent years; it took three clerks to carry in the letters at the subsequent hearing. Cahir recalls, "Every legislator in the Commonwealth was approaching me about "What is Quooshnet . . . Quonset . . .?" The House Ways and Means Committee, although they were in the midst of pulling together the fiscal 1988 budget, were sufficiently impressed to take the extraordinary step of holding the public hearing not in Boston, but in the Mashpee Town Hall. Over 150 citizens showed up for what legislators and local people alike later called the best organized meeting of its kind they had ever attended.

Cahir and his lower Cape counterpart, Representative Henri Rauschenbach, pointed out the importance of open space to the Cape and the state, and the necessity of protecting "whole ecosystems—not pieces."

Matt Patrick invoked the spirit of the Quashnet's most famous *habitué*, Daniel Webster, and reminded the legislators that, as a member of the same House of Representatives, his most important legacy was a bill protecting the state's fisheries.

Vernon Pocknett, past president of the Wampanoag Tribal Council, waxed poetic about the water—"Mother Earth's life blood." (After the meeting, the committee vice-chairman, Representative Angelo Scaccia of East Boston—one of the state's most urban districts—was seen, note pad in hand, quizzing Pocknett about his nature references and promising to use them on the House floor.)

There were speakers representing CPWB, the Research Reserve, the scientific community, the shellfish industry and the towns, but the finale fell to Fran Smith and the TU slide show. Smith flabbergasted some of the legislators with photos of 14-inch brook trout and much larger brown trout being released. "You put *that* back?" asked one incredulous politico. "Yes, sir, they're too valuable. We worked awfully hard to help produce that fish."

At the end Representative Scaccia called for testimony against the bill. None was offered. Representative Barbara Gray then called for a standing ovation for the TU volunteers. Soon after, House 5014 was attached to the Comprehensive Open Space Bill (House 5876) backed by Governor Michael Dukakis.

In November 1987, the bill was passed. Good news piled up as additional money was made available for protection of coastal rivers through the Division of Fisheries and Wildlife. In response, the Quashnet Coalition embarked upon the task of identifying key parcels of land for protection and having them appraised. The Quashnet-Waquoit Basin remains the priority, but other Cape watersheds are being looked at, too.

This new activity presents new problems in the volatile Cape Cod real estate market. As Vicki Lowell of the Falmouth 300 Committee points out: "You can spend several thousands of dollars on appraisal and by the time you're ready to purchase the land, it's obsolete." While the TU chapter and their allies confront this new challenge, one positive result which has already been secured is new recognition and respect for TU.

Vernon Pocknett acknowledges that, "My people pass through the Quashnet Valley all the time, just to see what you're doing. It's beautiful."

Vicki Lowell admits that, "We're not out in front on Waquoit Bay. We're following TU and CPWB."

Mashpee selectwoman Jean Thomas is "just getting to know the TU group, but they're great guys. The way that they're working, reading, expanding *themselves*, is just wonderful . . . With them I feel very comfortable. They have technical and scientific knowledge; they have initiative and drive."

Tom Cahir is "so impressed with their knowledge and intensity" and admits

171

he has "really become educated" through his association with Trout Unlimited.

Joe Bergin says, "They're now a major force environmentally on the entire Cape because of their tenacity on this project. They've gotten cooperation out of the towns we would never have expected. If TU speaks on a development project anywhere on the Cape, they're heard. I never expected that."

Ivan Valiela concurs: "You've got to give a lot of credit to people like TU. From taking out old tires to . . . this. There's tons of groups that clean up roadsides, etc. But when you get a group that can alter the course of planning, that's exciting."

Throughout the project's life, the leader has been Fran Smith, a Falmouth plumber originally from West Springfield, Massachusetts, on the edge of the Berkshires (Massachusetts' *real* trout country, the natives will tell you). When Uncle Sam dropped Fran off in the Falmouth area after a Vietnam stint, he did what any angler would do—he explored the local trout haunts. It happens that the closest trout stream to Otis Air Force Base was the Quashnet.

Smith also took time to read, from shiny new treatises on stream ecology and restoration to musty old volumes detailing the exploits of Daniel Webster and his cronies. One of them, Dr. Jerome V. C. Smith, wrote in 1833, that, "The various . . . places where the sea-trout are found are almost innumerable, for there is not a rivulet that flows from the springy banks of the land into the creeks of the salt marsh, but contains more or less." On the Quashnet, catches of a hundred trout might be made in an afternoon.

Fran's studies found their natural outlet in the Quashnet Restoration Project. What was an inaccessible piece of sucker water in 1975 today provides a first-class catch-and-release fishery for those in the know; and Fran has been the recipient of TU's National Trout Conservationist Award, as well as awards from the Heritage Conservation and Recreation Service and the United Nations Environment Programme.

But the job is nowhere near done, insists Fran. "If we finish the habitat restoration and don't reintroduce the original sea-run brook trout, then we haven't really accomplished anything." You can catch brook trout in the Quashnet today, and now and then a fish like Matt Patrick's 14 incher turns up. But, for practical purposes, the salter fishery no longer exists on any of the Cape streams.

The disappearance of the salter has perplexed Massachusetts fisheries biologists for years. One of them, James W. Mullan, speaking of the Mashpee River, suggested in a 1958 paper that, "Overstocking the river with hatchery-reared brook trout would result in a condition of overcrowding which would force the population of small native trout out to sea and they would thereby assume the anadromous habit."

Fran does not agree with Mullan's approach. Flying in the face of current fisheries biology orthodoxy, he feels that the salter is a genetically unique brook trout. "Everybody disagrees with me, but it's my feeling that there's something in the DNA—there's a spur there somewhere that makes them want to go to sea."

Mullan's experiment was tried in the Mashpee, the Quashnet and three other Cape streams between 1949 and 1956 and "worked" to the extent that the excess fish had to go somewhere, and some went to sea, even crossing open water to enter other rivers. But today there are no more salters than in 1949.

Rather than assuming that overpopulation is a precondition for anadromy (which is certainly not the case with other salmonids), one might hypothesize that the original decline in salters was due to pollution in the estuaries, where water quality has suffered far more than in the streams. The hardier brown trout may be better able to tolerate the contaminated estuaries than the brookies; they may also compete with them. Further, if one assumes that there is a genetic basis for anadromy in brook trout (as there appears to be in rainbow trout), then generations of isolation behind mill dams may have selected against the salter strain and in favor of nonmigratory fish (which have always been present). Further dilution of the tendency would have resulted from heavy stocking of hatchery fish derived from inland stock.

Now Fran wants to try *his* experiment: stocking the Quashnet with known sea-run brookies from a New Brunswick stream environmentally similar to the Quashnet. Arrangements have already been made to get the Canadian fish and, in 1983, Smith had targeted 1985 for the salter introduction. Now "I'm looking at a couple of years more of work, which will revolve around installation of devices— including very small deflectors to help us help Mother Nature's work."

If necessary, Fran would even favor the salters by eliminating the brown trout, a proposal which gives Joe Bergin apoplexy. For my part, I must admit that it is hard to give up the fantasy (occasionally realized) of tangling with a tackle-buster brown in an overgrown brook in favor of brook trout which might reach two and a half pounds at best.

Still, there are other places to fish for sea-run browns. Philosophically, Fran is right. He is not after just a place to fish. He is talking about ecological restoration in one of the most populous portions of our continent. As Mike Arritt puts it, "Any more the fish are almost secondary to restoring a river." That river, and the fish that live in it, are a barometer of the quality of life on Cape Cod. When the last grain of sand has run out of the Quashnet half of the hourglass, through the Moonakis and into the sea, Fran, Mike and company want that life, brook trout and all, to measure up to what Daniel Webster enjoyed.

Afterword: Preserving the Gift of Trout

Charles Gauvin

AMID MEMORIES ETCHED DEEP with the experience of fishing for trout in great settings, I must now reckon with an ever-shrinking angling calendar. Some may find it strange to read that the chief executive officer of the nation's largest salmonid conservation organization doesn't go trout fishing much anymore, but most of my trout-fishing experience these days is vicarious. It comes from meeting with, and sharing in the conquests and discoveries of, scores of avid (some would say rabid) anglers in the course of my work. None of this is to suggest, however, that my angling experience has become entirely troutless. Despite the press of business and the demands of family, including those of owning two Brittany spaniels—which ensure that any conflict between autumn fishing and hunting is resolved in favor of hunting—I still make time to fish for trout.

In my book, when it comes to choosing my fishing experiences, I have one basic rule: Wilder is better. Unfortunately, "wilder is better" doesn't apply much anymore to the places that we fish for trout. Sure, there are remote angling destinations like Alaska and Labrador, and we still can travel far from the nearest road to fish in the Rockies, Michigan's Upper Peninsula, and some parts of Maine. But, for most of us, with the compressive effect of business and family responsibilities, "wild" refers more to the fish we seek rather than the place in which we find them.

Even if much of our trout fishing occurs in places that are no longer truly "wild," the elemental role of nature distinguishes trout fishing from most other forms of recreation. Along with nature, history has played a commanding role in shaping the American trout-fishing experience. Centuries of technological development have gone into our fishing tackle, and European settlement has transformed many of the places where we put our gear to work. The fish we seek, some native and others of species not native to their habitat, have life histories that are unwritten sagas of behaviors in response to natural and human-caused stresses. In some places, trout fishing conjures up images of how things were when the term "ancient forest" described most of the North American continent; in others, such as our tailwater streams, it owes its very existence to the human alteration of nature. Fishing in either context places us within an ecological web, wrought by the confluence of human and natural history, whose connectedness determines the quality of the experience itself.

176

Trout-fishing aesthetics reinforce our sense of place within the web that encloses and defines our experience astream. I used to fish Maine's Kennebago River for the landlocked salmon that have run out of Mooslookmeguntic Lake every autumn since they were introduced to the Rangeley Lakes late in the nineteenth century. The river's drainage is predominantly industrial forest that has been cut over several times, but as I fish its spruce- and aspen-lined pools in my mind, warm September-lit hues beckon images of a primordial Northern Forest whose waters once spawned the giant native brook trout that today are the stuff of gigantic legends.

I also fish now and again in my mind a gentle bend of the Gallatin in Yellowstone Park, where I once shared the riverscape with a family of coyotes that had gathered on a small bluff beneath a draw that leads to the beyond of the Park's interior. As I probe the undercut bank in search of rainbows, the coyote family watches me from its perch among tufts of native grass, with whose blades the animals' coats blend perfectly. The coyotes' ancestors once watched as parties of white settlers crossed the Continental Divide, and the obsidian glimmer of their ancient eyes tracks my progress upstream through the next riffle.

When I contemplate my more recent trout-fishing experiences, one that stands out is the time that I have spent on the Delaware, especially the East Branch. If there is a stream that will always fill me with yearning, it is the East Branch. Because its trout are big and wild and can be finicky beyond belief, I know I'll never have enough of the East Branch.

I haven't even begun to invest the time necessary to acquire proficiency with, let alone mastery of, a river with half-mile-long pools and cruising fish that often seem to be ten feet farther than my best cast. Through saltwater angling, I have come to know the power of large fish, and yet the East Branch's fish always surprise me with their ability to take line. I'll never forget an incident that occurred several years ago when a colleague of mine stuck a large rainbow on a cold October afternoon. The fish screamed into the backing and then snared itself in a clump of weeds. He waded over to the trapped fish, gathering line as he approached, and reached into the dark water to effect what he thought would be a quick release. The release indeed proved to be a quick one when the big rainbow sensed its freedom to swim and overran the reel in a run that one would have expected from a bonefish, a bonito, or a bluefish.

Because my business involves thinking about the future of trout fishing in the wake of the human development that continues to overspread our nation, rivers like the East Branch now hold special appeal for me. Perhaps no great trout stream has so strong an urban connection. Its flows are dependent on the operating regime of New York City's water supply system, and its trout population ebbs and flows in response to human-caused environmental stresses in addition to nature's own random events. I step into the East Branch each spring wondering whether autumn and winter releases from Pepacton Reservoir have been sufficient to protect trout eggs and young-of-the-year fish in the river's channel, and whether there will be the same kind of insect life that was present the year before. In this respect, the East Branch is no different from hundreds of other streams around the country, streams whose flows and fish now exist on a slender precipice left by human engineering of our river systems. What distinguishes the East Branch for me is the wild fish that exist on that precipice.

Trout fishing is so steeped in the bucolic imagery of the frontier that it's easy to forget the largely man-made character of so many of our fisheries. Although the recent discovery of whirling disease has cracked the wild veneer on some of the West's premier streams, I'll wager that most visitors to the Madison still do not stop to consider that the Madison downstream from Hebgen Lake is a tailwater fishery whose ability to support a high-quality year-round population of trout over

177

so many river-miles is enhanced by releases from the dam. The same is probably true with respect to angler attitudes toward such popular fisheries as the South Platte and the Gunnison, as well as the San Juan and the Green—both of which were muddy, warm-water streams before they were dammed.

Does the pervasive human tinkering with our watersheds mean that streams now inhabited by trout are really no different from golf courses, that desirable angling conditions, once unmade, can be remade anew? I think not. Even if many of our trout streams are no longer sanctuaries of native aquatic biodiversity, most of those that have proved hospitable to wild trout probably could not be readily recreated and should be conserved. Countless others, whose habitat is limited by human alteration, warrant a good dose of restoration effort. Still, our ability to restore damaged streams should not lull us into believing that we can upset and once again recreate nature's balance.

Of trout fishermen, it is often said that "anglers are the first conservationists." There is commonsense truth in this. Those who fish for trout tend to become very passionate about the places they fish. Even in their altered states, trout streams still drain from the leading edges of our watersheds, from mountain passes left by the glaciers and from small springheads whose stortage can be millions of years old. Trout waters tend to be places of outstanding natural beauty, places that people want to conserve for their enjoyment and that of others. Trout fishermen value good habitat and beautiful surroundings, with the salutary result that many are willing to stand up and be counted when human activities threaten trout waters.

Despite the environmental setbacks that the 104th Congress would visit upon our waters in the name of "regulatory reform," I am confident that trout fishermen will continue to be a leading force for clean water and healthy habitat. We have accomplished a great deal over the past two decades, but the findings of a 1990 American Fisheries Society report—that almost 30 percent of all North American fishes, including a number of salmonids, are endangered, threatened, or of special concern—suggest that much remains to be done.

Much of what remains to be done involves better understanding and management not only of habitat, but of the genetic factors that comprise healthy native and wild trout and salmon. Our nation's trout and salmon species testify to the wonders of evolution. In the Pacific Northwest, there were once more than 400 uniquely adapted stocks of salmonids; waters in the Intermountain West teemed with a dozen or more bona fide subspecies of cutthroats; and biologists are just beginning to understand the evolutionary differences among the scores of remnant native brook trout populations east of the Mississippi. Yet, thanks to the legacy of habitat alteration and fish stocking, through which natural history and human history have collided, species biology has become confused, and entire species have lost their life history diversity through hybridization and introduction of exotic diseases. The loss of that life history diversity undermines the resiliency of salmonid species by depriving them of such traits as the ability to withstand natural and human-caused stresses like high water temperatures and sedimentation. It also extinguishes characteristics that anglers value, including fish size and weight.

Trout fishermen appreciate clearly the value of clean water and healthy habitat, but how much do they understand about the fish themselves? Thousands of anglers fish for "native" brown trout and rainbows in eastern, midwestern, and Rocky Mountain streams, in places where those fish may have become wild (self-sustaining), but never were native. Those fish that have become self-sustaining did not stop evolving when they were introduced to non-native habitats. Once there, they assumed the ecological niches formerly occupied by indigenous species.

We've come too far to "unscramble the eggs" in today's salmonid soufflé. I think that most anglers who have been sufficiently fortunate to fish over wild trout would agree that conserving gene pools, whether native or non-native, but wild, is the decisive element in ensuring the future of a quality angling experience. Imagine traveling to the Henry's Fork only to find it packed with the same stockers that mill about in the pond at the local trout club! But that hypothetical is too crude an example. With all the exotic species introductions in our waters, managing for wild fish sometimes is no easy matter. Sticky choices can arise between restoring native brook trout at the expense of established wild populations of non-native rainbows, or between restoring native squawfish and potentially harming wild rainbow and brown trout fisheries. Yet most of the conundrums exist only on the fringes, or in the minds of those who wish to erect roadblocks to wild fish conservation or restoration efforts. In most cases, "wilder is better" remains sound advice.

Trout Unlimited prides itself on having promoted a transition in fishery management from hatcheries to habitat, on having encouraged fishery biologists to be more than mere aquaculturists by focusing themselves and their budgets on the stream conditions and genetic factors that support healthy populations of native and wild salmonids. Although no one would dispute that the transition has begun to occur, I wonder how far we've really come. We have largely succeeded in educating anglers in "catch-and-release," yet at the same time that states like Montana and Pennsylvania began in the late 1970s to make major strides toward wild trout management, fishery managers in Washington State, Oregon, and California were stocking millions of hatchery salmon and steelhead in a vain effort to "supplement" runs of wild fish, with the result that returns of wild and hatchery fish plummeted, native gene pools disappeared, and precious funds that could have gone to habitat conservation went into a veritable "black hole."

A look at the raw numbers of salmonid "management" can be discouraging. Under the aegis of "sport fish restoration," millions of dollars flow annually from the federal government to the states. Yet, as my friend Ted Williams (Ted the writer, not the baseball luminary) has so poignantly asked, "Where are all the restored sportfish?" Trout Unlimited's recent study of the federal Sport Fish Restoration Fund found that fish hatcheries and stocking receive the lion's share of funding. Even where direct federal expenditures are involved, the U.S. Fish and Wildlife Service in recent years devotes 80 percent of its budget to hatcheries and fish stocking, and only a minuscule portion of those funds went toward wild fish restoration projects, as opposed to "put-and-take" and "put-and-grow" fisheries. With a few notable exceptions, the same pattern holds true for allocation of the funds that states raise through fishing license sales.

Lest I be branded a "hatchery basher," let me say that there is nothing inherently wrong with federal, state, and private entities spending money on hatcheries and stocking. Hatchery fish provide important recreational opportunities for millions of Americans in places where wild fish could not survive, let alone establish self-sustaining populations. Like much of everything else in life, however, it's a question of degree. The role that we trout fishermen play in answering that question—just as whether and how we answer the call to join in habitat conservation and restoration—will determine the future quality of our trout-fishing experience. There are times when we all must be vicarious anglers, but we can ill-afford to be vicarious conservationists.